Planned
Progeny

Planned Progeny

Shreyasi Prajaa

Dr. Parul Joshi

M. S. (*Ayu*) (*Prasutitantra Stri roga*)
M. D. (A. M.)
D. Y. Th. (Lucknow)
P. G. C. G. O. (Mumbai)
P. G. C. C. H. (Mumbai)
Diploma Research & Development
Diploma Hospital Management

PARTRIDGE
A Penguin Random House Company

To order additional copies of this book, contact
Partridge India
000 800 10062 62
orders.india@partridgepublishing.com

www.partridgepublishing.com/india

CONTENTS

In the name of ALLAAH The Most Beneficent and Merciful,
'We fashioned the things which clings into a chewed lump of
flesh and we fashioned the chewed flesh into bones and we
clothed the bones with intact flesh. Then we developed out of it
another creature. So blessed be ALLAH, the Perfect Creator.'
Holy Quran, *Sura Al-Muminun* (23:14)
[Unani Medicine for Women, Avicenna Research Publication, March 2003]

"Rasaat Raktam Tato Maamsm Maamsan Medah Prajaayate l
Medaso Asthi Tato Majjaa Majjah Shukrasya Sambhavah ll"
[*Sushruta Samhitaa, Sutra Sthaana,* Chapter 14/08]
"Evm maasen Rasa Shukram Bhavati Strinaam Cha Aartavam Iti ll"
[*Sushruta Samhitaa, Sutra Sthaana,* Chapter 14/09]

'Perfection is the true aim of all culture, the spiritual, psychic, mental
and vital and it must be the aim of our physical culture also.
Human body is the means of fulfillment of *dharma* and
dharma means every ideal which we can propose to ourselves
and the law of its working out and its action.
A total perfection is the ultimate aim which we set before us, for our
ideal is the Divine Life which we wish to create here, the life of the Spirit
fulfilled on earth, life accomplishing its own spiritual transformation
even here on earth in the conditions of the material universe.
That can materialize only when the body also undergoes a transformation'.
[Sri Aurobindo, 'The Supramental Manifestation', SABCL Vol. 16, Pg. 5]

PREFACE

It was in 1978 (at age 18) when I first met my *Vidyaa Guru* Dr. Mrs. Ila Deshpande. She insisted on my accompanying in her endeavour for female health and healthy progeny. At that age all I could do was to follow her. Slowly but steadily under her guidance I started understanding the depth of Ayurvedic literature. Luckily during this span of over 32 years, I have had multilayered prosperous exposures. I came across various books, booklets and magazine articles on the subject. Much has been said, yet there are many unattended questions. Some of these questions have been handled by the main *Ayurveda* texts in a very simple manner but the language is *Sanskrit*. Thus a need was felt for a comprehensive road-map to planned pregnancy as per the literature and present scenario.

The booklet aims at helping young couples to achieve their goal of "*Shreyasi prajaa* i.e. Child of dreams" and fulfillment of social obligation. Society is equally responsible for each child that starts taking shape both in the to-be-parent's minds and its mother's womb hence the title given is 'Planned progeny'.

Since medicines cannot be dictated, the booklet does not contain the medicine part of the subject. My field experience is: a clear definite approach is very much more important than medical dependency.

This booklet is only a guide, yet I have tried to cover as many points possible, so that it may help as a handbook for future researchers.

Author is very much thankful to all who helped conceive and fulfill this dream project of Dr. Mrs. Ila S. Deshpande. I would love to mention Prof. Kireet Joshi, Prof. P. V. Tewari and Dr. Usha for their tender and fruitful guidance. I owe a lot to Dr. Miss S. C. Pandya, my *Maa, Maasibaa*; dear grandmothers *Shantubaa* and *Vajiyaabaa*. I heartedly thank my sunna Gaurang for all the help and care.

Since the book is based on *Ayurveda*, the main words are in *Sanskrit* and so marked by *italic*. Their relevant English words are given in bracket.

Parul

CHAPTER 1
Planning a pregnancy

Importance of planned pregnancy:

India is a country with a divergent multi-faced cultural heritage. Every caste and clan has its own rituals, yet there is oneness. Weather differs and so does the nature of people, yet we Indians have a strong oneness. This oneness is in: certain basic beliefs, lifestyles, approach to life and so the contents of Ayurvedic texts have not needed a change over the centuries even with generations of new physicians and new technologies. But then what is 'That' which still remains to be understood and implemented? There are scores of points, but we will concentrate on 'Healthy Progeny'; 'Child of Dreams'.

Human nature, the world over, is the same since time immemorial and this truth is true in case of the present scenario of progeny and related problems.

While visiting an unknown place, a proper guide and necessary equipments, make the journey comfortable and pleasant.

Human life is precious. Indian social life has multi-faced responsibilities. There are many expectations from a child by the parents, family and society; fulfillment of which helps maintain a healthy society.

A couple dreams of many things. Some of them contradict each other even without their knowledge. This thought conflict leads to confusion which endangers fulfillment of the dreams.

The booklet aims to create a road-map for such to-be-parents for obtaining a progeny of their dreams.

The points are very simple and easy to practice.

Some of these points are still in practice.

In the present times of nuclear family type, the rules for maintaining health (*Svastha-vritta, Sada-vritta*) are all the more helpful. We can call them 'golden rules' of health for self, family and society at large.

We have to keep in mind that: 'humanity remains healthy if every human is healthy'.

The environment i.e. air, water, soil; plants, trees, birds, animals, insects etc.; atmosphere, thoughts, feelings, etc. remain healthy and positive only if the people residing there are conscious and healthy.

With these concepts in mind, we proceed along the road to 'healthy conception and child of dreams'.

Care taken by the couple:

The importance of physico-psychological health and potency are known. Any thing that disturbs them should be solved before conception. Human life and begetting is a complex process. There are no short cuts. *Ayurveda* has given a highway for health and healthy progeny, but keeping oneself on road and attaining the desired goal requires determination, patience and perseverance.

Basic expectations from the couple:

The idea to have a child and its qualities should be clear before marriage.

Male factors: he should be interested, has feelings for his partner, is of proper age (25 to 40 years), has good physique (neither *heena anga* nor *adheeka anga*) and health, has good intelligence and understanding; is pleasant natured; does not have vices like tobacco, wine, etc.; has purified his body by following health rules and required medicines; has purified his *mana*, longings and thoughts by constant meditations and self-suggestions.

Female factors: she should be interested, has feelings for her partner, is of proper age (20 to 35 years), is physically and emotionally healthy, has good intelligence and understanding; is able to understand husband's needs; is from a different family clan (*atulya gotra*), has good physique (neither *heena angi* nor *adheeka angi*), has healthy menstruation and ovulation; is pleasant natured and pleasant mannered; does not have vices like tobacco, wine etc.; has purified her body by following health rules and required medicines; has purified her *mana*, longings and thoughts by constant meditations and self-suggestions.

Expected qualities of to-be-parents: they should not be of too small or too old age; they should not have chronic or long standing physical disease, mental, psychological, psycho-sexual disorders. They should avoid habit of not attending natural calls properly; avoid misbelief and superstition. They should not be recently bereaved due to some loss etc. Those having habit of food made from single taste for a long time; have over eaten; have wrong food habits since a long time; who have not purified themselves; have wrong life style habits, who are in a wrong (other than classical) physical posture (during copulation) are to refrain from immediate conception.

A lady who has not matured (physically / mentally / emotionally), is too old, remains dirty; is stressed, depressed, angry or afraid; has any chronic disease (physical or functional) specifically related to the genitals; has not purified herself satisfactorily, does not want a child, should avoid conception.

It will be accepted by all that couples go for a conception only on attaining due health in the larger interests.

Importance of parental age:

Starting conjugal life and planning a family come only on completion of studies and having a proper and steady source of income with stability in career. The idea being they are mentally and physically prepared to bear the responsibility of up-bringing a child.

For Male:

Proper age for fatherhood is neither before 25 nor after 60 years; 25 to 40 being most appropriate.

Reasoning: Before 25 years his body is itself undergoing growth hence it may not be able to bear the burden of conjugal life and giving a potent baby. After the age of 40 years, his body starts undergoing catabolic changes. From age 60 to 69 *Vaardhakya* the phase meaning completion of middle age starts. This indicates entering the *Vaanaprastha-ashram* i.e. recession from worldly activities. At 70 a male is supposed to accept *Sanyaasa* i.e. leave worldly life for bettering his life after death.

Rebuilding the four *aashrama* type of life is very much the need of the hour.

For Female:

Proper age for motherhood is on completion of 18 (but only when normal menstruation is stabilized) and before 40 years. Earlier than 18, her body is in the growth phase hence it may not be able to bear the burdens of conjugal life, pregnancy, child birth and upbringing. In the present times she starts having degenerating changes from 30 years which disturbs the quality and potency of her child. Normally a female starts undergoing catabolic changes after 35 years which can increase the risk of fetal abnormalities. Age 40 to 45 is onset of menopausal changes i.e. a period of definite imbalances hence there are ample of chances for abortion or congenital deformities.

Importance of completion of studies and income steadiness:

Healthy conjugal life is sum of lives of two individuals. A stressed couple cannot be healthy.

Indian culture divides lifecycle into 4 *aashramas* viz. 1) *Brahmacharya-aashrama*, 2) *Gruhastha-aashrama* 3) *Vaanaprastha-aashrama* and 4) *Sanyaasa-aashrama*.

A child is allowed to enter the *Brahmacharya-aashrama* for starting his studies on completion of age 5 years or on attainment of a proper socialized behaviour. A *brahmachaari* enters the *Gruhastha-aashrama* on completion of studies and having a reasonable source of income with a clear motive of having a family. This was supposed to be achieved between age 25 to 30 years. The gateway to *Gruhastha-aashrama* is *Vivaaha samsakaara*. This includes *Laajaa homa, Putreshti yagna, Garbhaadhaana-samsakaara* etc. rituals which very specifically teach the couple their duties and social expectations from them. There are specific rules to be observed by the couple immediately after marriage which include fasting, taking specific medicines to purify mind and body. Wife has to observe certain rules during menstruation, ovulation; they meet on specific constellation nights to beget child of their dreams. It all requires income steadiness.

General rules for the couple:

Though each couple is individually different, there are common rules to be followed for maintenance of physical, mental and emotional basic health. *Ayurveda* calls them basic health rules. They include observing *Deenacharyaa* (schedule observed during day), *Ritu charyaa* (season wise life schedule), *Maithuna charyaa* (conduct during cohabitation), *Sada-vritta* (general rules of individual behaviour), *Sada-achaara* (general rules of social conduct). Detailed discussion of these rules is abundant in texts of *Ayurveda*.

Food:
Does:

Traditional family diet, rich in cow's milk and *ghee* (made from buttermilk), which is easy to digest, has all the six tastes with dominance of sweet taste.

Seasonal vegetables and fruits are taken with due care to ensure their easy digestion, assimilation and body acceptance.

Frequent use of vegetables like Gourd (*Dudhi*), Corm of Amarphophallus campanulatus Blume (*Surana*), Drumstick (*Saragavo, Shigru*), Green amaranth (*Tendulia; Taandaliya)*; pulses like green Gram (*Moong, Mudga*);

Cereals like rice (*Shashtheeka* variety, Oryza sativa), *Yava* (*Java*, Hordeum vulgare); fruits like ripe Mango (*Keri, Aamra*), Pomegranate (*Daadima*), Banana (*Kelaa*), Sugar cane (*Sheradi*), Grapes (*Draakshaa*), Jujuba (*Bora, Badara*), Red date (*Kharjura*), Rose apple (*Jaamun*), Fig (*Anjeera*), Grewia asiatica (*Phaalsa*), Mulberry *(Shetur)*; dry fruits like Fig, Grapes, Buchanamia seeds (*Chironji*), Date (*Kharjura*), Jujuba (Red date; *Badara).*

Take curd or buttermilk made from cow's milk only after adding black Pepper, Cumin seeds, Saffron or Cardamom.

Use sugar crystals instead of routine sugar (as it is easy to digest).

Use honey where ever possible.

Vegetarian diet helps.

Six factors that compose and influence a foetus:

Maataa	*Pitaa*	*Aatmaa*	*Saatmya*	*Rasa*	*Satva*
Mother	**Father**	**Self**	**Acceptable**	**Chyle of mother**	**Inner self**
Skin	Scalp hair	Psyche	Non laziness	Proper growth	Devotion
Blood	Moustache	Intuition	Voice	Tie up of the	Character
Muscles	Beard	Memory	Contents of	Soul	Cleanliness
Fat	Axillary	Figure	the senses	Putting on	Hate
Umbilicus	and Pubic	Voice	Colour of	weight	Memory
Heart	hair	Body colour	body	Getting proper	Indulgence
Pancreas	Skin hair	Feelings	Potency	nourishment	Renounce
Spleen	Teeth	Craving	Enthusiasm	Understanding	Evil desire
Liver	Bones	Hate	Getting	Content	Valor
Urinary	Arteries	Activity	lured	Retirement	Fright
bladder	Veins	Decisive power	Immunity	Enthusiasm	Anger
Small	Tendons	Thinking	Ideal brain		Transitional
and large	Semen	Co-ordination	power		sleep
intestines		Ego	Vigour		Enthusiasm
Rectum		Perseverance	Satisfaction		Sharpness
with		Sense organs	Initiation		Softness
orifice		Anger			Faith
Bone		Greed			Thankfulness
marrow		Passion			Manners
Stomach		Fright			Intelligence
Uterus		Jealousy			Occupation
		Obeying/			Seriousness
		breaking rules			Memory
		Respiration			
		Voiding			
		Knowledge			
		about self			

Don'ts

Avoid spicy, sour, chilly, fried, fermented, preserved and chilled foods.

Avoid foods known to be of poor quality, bad taste and odour.

Avoid foods not used by the predecessors of both families e.g. non-vegetarian diet in family with vegetarian habits.

Avoid chilled beverages and refrigerated food items even fruits or juices.

Avoid mixing milk with curds or butter milk; avoid taking milk with sour and fermented foods or food containing salt, fruits, garlic, onion, etc. which changes the chemistry of milk and makes it harmful. Avoid taking cooked with uncooked foods, *ghee* with honey in equal quantity (in short: *Ayurvediya viruddha aahaara*).

Avoid taking curd and curd products like *Shrikhand* (churned curd with sugar), *Mattha* (churned curd or plain yogurt), *Lassi* (churned curd with 5 to 10% of water or a blend of yogurt, water and powders of spices like black pepper, roasted cumin seeds, cumin and coriander) etc. after sunset.

Avoid frequent use of sweets made from *Maava* (dried whole milk).

Never use heated honey, castor oil or curds orally, as heat induces harmful chemical changes in them.

Habits: (*Deenacharyaa*)
Does:

Wake up 2 hours before sunrise (*Brahma muhurta*), pay proper attention to natural urges i.e. form habit of attending natural calls in time, in proper position, with due concentration on attending them.

Dantadhaavana: Clean teeth (if possible) with tender twig of Indian lilac (*Neem*), Bullet wood (Spanish cherry, *Bakula*), Banyan tree (*Vata*), Indian beech (*Karanja*), Cutch tree (Acacia, *Baaval*), etc. which clean and protect teeth, oral cavity and throat also.

Jihvaanirlekhana: Clean tongue up to the hind part with a tongue cleaner.

Kavalagrahana: Perform gargles with warm water. Water should reach hind part of tongue and epiglottis so that it cleans mouth, throat and hind part of nose as well.

Ushahpaana: Drink water from a (covered) copper pot kept overnight. Water should be drunk slowly, in a comfortable sitting posture.

Chidra Samrakshana: (The procedure is done during early hours of dawn)

Keep all orifices (ears, throat, anus, urinary meatus and vagina in females) clean and lubricated (like applying castor oil over anus or around urethral orifice);

Instill warm cow's *ghee* (made from butter) 6 to 8 drop in both nostrils (when it reaches mouth spit it and clean mouth with warm water) in a lowered head-straight lying posture. Don't allow *ghee* to go down the throat.

Sesame oil (oil should be warm i.e. body temperature) 4 to 6 drop in each ear in a comfortable-side lying posture with legs kept straight. After 3 to 5 minutes when oil has seeped to the mid ear, plug the external auditory orifice with sterile cotton wool taking care that size of the plug is larger to orifice. Take care to remove these plugs after 2 to 3 hours.

Abhyanga: Apply warm oil (sesame or mustard according to season) over body; specifically folds and joints.

Ubatana: Apply paste of flour of *besan* or *yava* and skin care handy herbal powders like Turmeric, Sandal, Saffron, Rose petals and Rose water or *ark* all over body followed by gentle message. This removes dirt, stimulates blood supply and provides nourishment to skin and underlying tissues, which increases whole body cell immunity.

Snaana: Take bath with warm or hot water (according to season and atmosphere). Where ever possible leaves of Indian lilac (*Neem*), Vitex negundo (*Nirgundi*), etc. are put into the water before heating it to benefit from their properties. Take bath regularly.

Dry the whole body thoroughly with coarse cotton cloth.

Vastra (Clothes): Wear properly fitting, comfortable under garments and clothes designed according to prevalent season, type of work and life style.

Cloth material may be cotton, silk, jute etc. natural body friendly yarns such that it absorbs sweat easily.

Cloth colour should be sober and cheerful with psycho friendly design.

Avoid dark or black colored synthetic clothes with meaningless writings or designs.

Anulepana: Paste of Sandal or Bhasma is applied over forehead, arms, above elbow, chest and neck. This acts as protection against various infections (viruses and Ayurvedic *Graha* group of infective disorders).

Offer prayers.

Praatah-aahaara (Breakfast): As per season, digestion, body needs and in time.

On returning from work wash both hands, legs and face properly and change clothes.

Always wash hands before eating even while using spoon, fork and knife. However eating with fingers stimulates appetite and prompts digestion.

Paadatraana sevana (Footwear): Wear comfortable footwear i.e. which does not bite, squeeze or is loose fitting, hard or uneven. Main aim of footwear is to protect the feet hence they are related with foot and leg health.

Kshaura-karma (Shave): Keep moustache and beard properly trimmed and in proper shape. Axillary and pubic hair should be removed every five days with sterile razor. Avoid chemicals. Alum application after shaving helps prevents bleeds, irritation and infections.

Don'ts:

Avoid waking up after sun-rise.

Avoid untidiness, irregularity, hasty or no bath.

Avoid not having Faith.

Avoid going out bare footed or wearing hard, uncomfortable footwear because all body points are located in feet.

Avoid keeping long untidy hair.

Aahaara vidhi (Proper way of eating):

Does:

Eat with full concentration on: type, quality, quantity of food, water and other liquids; food should be taken in a pleasant atmosphere,

Food should be served by dedicated caring satisfied person (who has taken enough food).

Eating in small morsels is advised.

Morsel should be swallowed only after chewing it thoroughly (i.e. when it turns liquid).

Proper time of eating is: when hunger is felt but a fixed time is advisable.

Preferable posture while eating is *Padmaasana. Thaali* (dish) be placed at a comfortable height (so that morsel can be taken easily).

Some houses have a routine of decorating eating place with flowers, rangoli or *Alpanaa*. Diet depends upon the quality of hunger (yet a quantity has to be determined).

Don'ts:

Avoid eating in unfriendly untidy place with too loud and stress inducing noises or music.

Avoid taking food irregularly, very less quantity or infrequently.

Frequent and over eating disturb the digestive process hence are avoided.

Avoid too much dry or too many liquids as they hinder proper digestion and assimilation.

Avoid taking food in an uncomfortable posture and while suppressing natural urges.

Any type of stress or strain during or after food leads to harmful chemical changes which can be eliminated by whole body purification processes only.

Avoid taking alcohol, tobacco etc. (they reduce fertility and lead to birth of a thirsty, restless child having less memory).

Avoid taking food when thirsty and drinking liquids or water when hungry as that disturbs the functioning of digestion.

Working or sleeping immediately after food disturbs the digestive and assimilation process.

Nivaasa Sthaana (Type of residence) or *Kaaryaalaya* (Office):

Does:

Try and stay in warm dry place during monsoon or humid climate; in warmth during winter and in cool humid atmosphere during summer.

The place, its atmosphere and environment should be friendly.

The seat should be comfortably soft, accommodative, steady, the height being comfortable so that the working remains comfortable for hands, back and legs.

In people with laborious type of work, intermittent rest is advised to avoid fatigue and accumulation of unfriendly chemicals.

Don'ts:

Avoid staying in humid, chilled atmosphere devoid of sunlight and free air-flow.

Avoid unfriendly environment as it creates sense of unsafety (most inappropriate place for a child of dreams).

Avoid unbalanced sitting posture, too high or low, too hard or soft, uneven, uncomfortable, unsteady seat or chair e.g. revolving chair on wheels.

Avoid retaining urine, stool, flatus, hunger, thirst, sleep, tears and yawning etc. physical urges.

Avoid excessive, irregular, improper physical exercises or no exercise (*avyaayaama*).

Avoid getting fatigued.

Vyavahaara (Behaviour):

Does:

Speak well

Practice Truth

Behave politely

Give respect to elderly etc.

Have Faith

Be helpful

Try and maintain positivity in personal thoughts, speech and behavior.

Be clear and balanced in thoughts and actions.

Maintain punctuality.

Maintain cleanliness and neatness.

Don'ts:

Avoid being quarrelsome, critical, sorrowful, nervous (leads to lean or weak child)

Avoid excessive thinking, torturing others (leads to jealous or genitally weak child)

Excessive indulgence (sex) (leads to weak, congenital problems or genitally weak child)

Avoid excessive laziness and sleep (leads to sleepy, less intelligent child who suffers from loss of appetite)

Paryaavarana (Environment):

Does:

Your house should be well ventilated and having enough assess to sunlight.

Maintain pleasant, cheerful atmosphere inside the house specially the bedroom.

Colors: light yellow, pink, green or sky blue (keeps mind and mood pleasant).

Light entertaining Indian music; in case of *raga,* its proper selection and time of playing helps maintain cheerfulness and freshness. Select a sober useful *raga* which creates positive currents.

Bed should be strong, still, of proper size, well designed, comfortable, having facility for mosquito net, properly placed i.e. in east-west direction, away from door and window; mattress should be soft, comfortable and of proper size.

Try and stay between helpful, supportive, elderly, experienced people.

Be eco-friendly i.e. grow plants specifically fruit trees, flowering creepers having flowers with pleasant smell and cheerful colours; have pets, give grains and water to birds etc.

Don'ts:

Avoid hostile, unfriendly home and bedroom atmosphere.

Avoid seeing hostility or horrific scenes, beating or unfriendly behavior, peeping into well or deep valley (they lead to abortion).

Avoid riding a jumpy or unbalanced vehicle or road.

Avoid listening to high pitched sound or excessive exposure to shrill, harsh, panicky voices or sounds.

All disease causing factors a couple practices makes their child prone to those diseases.

In short:

A couple should consciously avoid:

1) everything that disturbs oneself, partner, environment and specifically their thoughts,
2) Anything and everything that hinders incoming of a healthy child.

Importance of healthy semen (*Shukra shudhdhi*):

It is understood that a child of dreams is physically strong and potent. Strength and potency are inherited from semen (*shukra*). Semen includes spermatozoa and fluid medium.

Healthy semen is white or transparent, smells and tastes sweet, its consistency is thick, is slimy and unctuous in touch, is abundant in quantity and does not create burning, pain or itching sensation during ejaculation (gets ejaculated without any pain or effort and is in enough quantity).

There are many faults found in semen (*Shukra dooshti*). Some are:

1) Foul smell (*kunapa gandhi*): smells like decaying corpse
2) Pus like appearance (*pooti pooya nibham*): appears like pus
3) Knotted appearance (*granthibhoota*): agglutinated
4) Insufficient quantity (*ksheena*): ejaculate and count are less than required amount
5) Stool urine mingled smell (*mootra purisha gandhee*): ejaculate smells like urine, stool or both. There are various theories about the cause and treatment.
6) *Vaata dushta*: ejaculate is frothy, thin, less unctuous, is less potent.
7) *Pitta dushta*: ejaculate is blue or yellow in colour, passes with burning sensation, may contain blood and is less potent.
8) *Kapha dushta*: ejaculate is white, thick, slimy, viscous, is less potent.

Semen with these defects is not capable of fertilizing the ovum and so conception does not occur. In case conception occurs, embryo being weak cannot get embedded and develop; if it grows, premature birth of a baby with less vitality is born. There is a high chance of chromosomal or genetic deformity e.g. if the male procreating elements in the sperm are afflicted, the offspring may be sterile; if only a part of the chromosome or genetic factor is affected, the male genitals or their functions will be affected, etc.

Thus faulty semen is responsible for troubles to child and wife

"*Shukram he dushtam saapatyam sdaaram baadhate narah*".

Important rules for the male partner:

A male is compared with seed (*Beeja bhoota smrutah pumaana*).

Along with the general health rules, male has to observe cohabitation rules while taking due care to regularly use drugs that maintain potency of his semen (*vajikara sevana*). It is for the person to understand his importance in begetting child of dreams. The way a weak seed though sown (*beeja bhoota smrutah pumaana*) in a fertile land is unable to sprout and grow into a fruitful tree, weak semen does not give a healthy and potent child.

Indian literature has ample of examples on options to have a healthy child in such circumstances.

Important rules for the female:

A female is compared with earth (*Kshetra bhoota smrutah naari*).

She has the power to beget a strong healthy desired child (even in adverse circumstances); by following simple rules during menstruation, ovulation, copulation, on confirmation of fruitful copulation, during pregnancy, during labour, post-partum and even during breast feeding, she has the strength to bring desired changes.

Rajaswalaa Paricharyaa: (Rules for woman during menstruation)

'*Rajaswalaa*' is: (1) female in the menarche (12 years) to menopause (50 years) age group [for conception ideal age is 20 to 35 years] and
　　　　　　　(2) female during menstruation (periods).

Menstruation and ovulation are controlled by *Apaana vaayu*. Maintained equilibrium of *Apaana vaayu* is mandatory to have a healthy menstruation, ovulation, conceptus, fetus and baby. Thus observing both *Rajaswalaa* and *Rutumati paricharyaa* maintain equilibrium of *Apaana vaayu* and help beget a potent, healthy progeny.

Shuddha aartava (Properties of normal menstrual blood):

Quantity: neither too much nor too less (*Chaturanjali pramaanam*-own 4 handfuls)

Inter menstrual period: 28 to 30 days (*Chandra maasa; yathaa kaale*)

Duration: 5 to 7 days (*Pancha raatra anubandhi*)

Colour index: bright red (*Asruk*) to bluish or blackish red (*Ishat krushnam*)

Other properties: devoid of stickiness, comes without pain, burning or itching; does not come as clots (*Nish pichchu daaha arti*); has smooth flow like normal urination or defecation; soiled clothes get cleaned with water.

Any alterations in these criteria denote vitiation which has to be cleared before conception with proper medications.

Rajaswalaa Paricharyaa (Rules to be observed during menstruation):
(Rules in addition to those quoted earlier: so that physiology is maintained)

It is known that menstrual and ovarian cycles are interlinked and both are inter-dependent on the emotional status of lady.

Does:

Food: Eat meals made from *Shaali* (red type) rice, barley, cow's milk, cow's *ghee*, in short easily digestible, limited quantity and liquid type of food to be consumed in a vessel made from gold, silver, brass or glass.

Follow rules of healthy eating.

Habits: Observe abstinence; try to stay away from various types of strong emotions.

Practice cleanliness: regarding body, clothes, undergarments, pads, etc.

Wear clean fumigated clothes especially under garments and change pads frequently.

Sleep on straight, comparatively hard floor. If possible use *Darbha* (Desmotachya bipinnata, a type of grass), coir or jute mattress. Try to avoid regular bedding to avoid the menstrual odour.

Don'ts:

Avoid frequent eating or over eating.

Avoid spices, chilies, salty or use of any single taste.

Avoid cold, refrigerated, food with bad smell and taste.

Avoid sleeping during day.

Avoid sitting or sleeping on floor, in damp, cold places or exposure to scorching heat.

Avoid use of mascara (medicated *kaajal*), ablation, taking tub bath, taking head bath, adoring with fragrant flowers, ornaments, etc.

Avoid shredding tears, oil massage, nail paring, running fast, having vigorous exercise, exertion, laughing loudly, talking too much, listening to loud harsh music; coarse or harsh sound, sitting or sleeping in strong wind especially from the east direction.

Avoid all types of purifications like *panchkarma* (especially *vamana*-emesis and *nasya*), *praanayaama* etc.

Utensils used for cooking and eating should be unbroken.

Importance of these rules: to ensure proper menstruation.

A healthy menstruation washes the uterus and enhances development of healthy endometrium (inner most mucous skin of uterus) necessary for healthy embedment and fetal growth. It also helps stimulate healthy ovulation.

Table: Rules for lady during 1 to 4 days of menstruation:

Does	Don'ts
Abstinence	Coitus, undue excitement
Regular Liquid Nutritive Freshly prepared food having all six tastes	Taking heavy to digest, dry, single taste, rotten or chilled preserved food
Maintain cleanliness: local, general; pads, clothes, bedding etc.	Remain soiled, not changing pads frequently, use of strong perfumes or deodorants to suppress body odour
Maintain calm Avoid exertion and stress	Weeping, excessive stress or strain, exposure to emotional setbacks, exercises, running, hearing loud harsh unpleasant sounds, seeing horrific scenes, etc.
Wear comfortable underwear and clothes as per the season	Wearing tight fitting, very bright or gloomy coloured clothes having injurious chemicals and yarn
Avoid beutificants	Using different beutificants, creams or *lepam*
Take enough rest during day and sleep during night, maintain punctuality	Sleeping during day, not attending natural calls properly or in time
Avoid any type of *dosha* provocative activity	*Abhyanga*-oil massage, taking classical bath, head bath, *panchkarma*, *nasya*, blood donation
Stay in a comfortable place	Stay in strong winds; sitting or sleeping in cold damp places
In case of problem consult an expert in time.	

Avoid sex during periods because:

Day of menstruation	Effect of sex on conceptus and outcome of pregnancy
Day I	Phantom-pregnancy (*Vaata garbha*), Child having short-life (*Anaayushya*), Abortion (*Sraava* or *Paata*)
Day II	Death in post-natal period (initial 10 days)
Day III	Congenital physical abnormalities (*Asampoornaanga*), having less life span (*Alpaayusha*)

Day IV (taken head bath)	Complete fetus (*Sampoornaanga*), having long-life (*Deerghaayushya*)

Importance of observing rules during menstruation:

Sr. No.	Mother practices	Possible outcome
1	Day sleeping	Sleepy child
2	Applies collyrium in eyes	Blind or child with impaired vision
3	Shredding tears	Child having defective eyesight
4	Classical bathing or use of beutificants	Leads a miserable life
5	Anointing body (*Abhyanga*)	Affected with obstinate skin disease
6	Paring nails	Bad nails or problems related to nails
7	Running or hasty walking	Restless child
8	Excessive laughter	Brown teeth, palate and tongue
9	Excessive talking	Tiresomely talkative child
10	Hearing loud unpleasant sounds	Deaf
11	Combing hair	Baldness
12	Excessive tiring work	Insanity

Important general rule: Which-ever organ or system representing part of the ovum gets disturbed; shall disturb the corresponding organ or system of the child to be born out of that ovum.

A healthy menstruation leads to proper ovulation which tends to lead to a healthy and proper fertilization and implantation; these are the necessary steps for a Healthy progeny.

The couple has to observe abstinence till completion of menstruation period. Coitus during these days is either unfruitful, leads to abortion or premature birth with a high chance of fetal morbidity, decreases local immunity which makes them susceptible to various genital diseases.

Rutumati (a woman in ovulation i.e. days 6 to 18 post-menstruation)

During *Rutu kaala* (period of fertility) internal and external os of cervix-uteri remain patent. Vaginal pH remains alkaline. This helps sperm penetration. Once this period is over, vaginal pH becomes acidic and the cervical os closes. Thus recognizing and utilizing this period is very much important for the to-be-parents.

This phase varies according to brought up, life style, season, food and emotional status of woman at the particular time.

How to recognize the 'fertility time'?

She looks bright, cheerful, feels cheerful, she feels her face, mouth, teeth moist and sticky, feels interested, likes to talk and hear about her husband, feels her thighs, buttocks, abdomen flanks, eye lids and hair relaxed, feels a special flutter, a twitching sensation in arms, pelvic part, umbilicus, thighs, hips, breasts and calf part of legs.

These signs and symptoms described in *Ayurveda* texts are experienced by a self-conscious woman and coincide with Sonography findings of ovulation.

This is the most appropriate time for cohabitation and conception.

Milk treated with *Jeevaniya* group of drugs is given to preserve her vaginal softness, moisture and pH value.

Rutumati Paricharyaa (generally days 6 to 18 post-menstruation) [Rules to be observed from completion of menstruation to end of ovulation period]

Does	Don'ts
Take classical and head bath, wear ornaments, wear flowers or garlands having pleasant fragrance and cheerfully colored, wear well designed, properly fitting clothes, with material as per the prevalent season, offer prayers, make offerings, give alms and be helpful	Stay dirty, tense, disorderly; wear tight fitting dress or that not in accordance with prevalent season or family status; not having faith in Almighty, being arrogant and disrespectful
See, think, read or stay at a place which helps create and maintain an atmosphere befitting the child of dreams	Anxiety, exertion, stress, see and think of horrible, unfriendly things. All types of negative feelings, porn etc. exciting films
Maintain genital health, lubricate them daily with Castor, Sesame or Coconut oil and pour warm water over the whole part	Abusing genitals with masturbation, toys or unnatural sex, excessive indulgence, be unfaithful to partner

Have sex in a pleasant friendly atmosphere only on successful completion of physical and mental cleansing procedures	Go to an unknown unfriendly place; go out late in night; go for a child "unplanned"
Remain conscious about diet, behaviour, maintain cleanliness of body: specifically genitals, clothes: specifically under-garments; atmosphere, thoughts and emotions	Excessive indulgence, take non conventional, high fat or unhygienic food in large quantity or frequently that create indigestion
Meeting at: proper well-planned time; posture; at a comfortable pre-prepared place rid of unnecessary intrusions but within the eyesight of friendly elders and experienced Physician	Not respecting: good health, behaviour and conduct rules; cohabitation rules e.g. during dawn, dusk, on full moon or wrong constellation nights, in unpleasant mood or unfriendly place
Properly cleansed female is given diet prepared in sesame oil and black gram. Male is given more of milk, honey, curds, cow's *ghee* and rice or *yava kheera* with (*Shukra vruddhi* + *Sruti kara*) Spermatogenic, vitalizing drugs in the morning and *Shaali* rice with milk in the evening: milk used should be from a white cow having an alive and healthy white calf	Use of spices, chilies, tobacco, soft or strong chilled drinks, not having a confused picture about the type of child they are planning
Couple has and maintains feelings, faith and respect for each other. They have good understanding and harmony	Have disputes, loss of mutual faith, cannot maintain harmony
Couple having taken proper diet mounts a decorated comfortable bed, husband with right leg and wife with left leg. Position of the partners should be supine for female with the male comfortably climbed over her.	Any other position like the male below, side ways or in uncomfortable postures which do not allow proper and complete vaginal deposition of semen
Couple tries and refrains from any negative feelings. They maintain mutual co-ordination and with full concentration in their aim of healthy desired dream child-perform	Excessive use of salts, medical emesis, stay hungry, thirsty, afraid, anxious or grief stricken etc. negative feelings

It is known that food, thoughts and frequent remembering help a woman achieve child of dreams—in physique, psychological and behaviour status also.

Lady who does not observe these rules: may be due to ignorance, laziness or sheer chance; harms her fetus and cannot accomplish her project of 'dream child'.

Couple having cohabitation after completion of fertility time is only for sexual pleasure. Such cohabitation remains unfruitful.

Ayurveda texts emphasize that all couples go for a planned pregnancy to repay social obligation. The above stated rules do not only help in sex selection, but can also give the desired skin color, color of iris, body build-up, nature, behavior, physical strength; mental attitude and strength, etc. points to their child. Quality of the un-born child is totally in the hands of to-be-parents hence the importance of the purified woman first seeing her husband after completion of menstruation. Pre-conception sex selection is actually advocated for a potent child. Every child has a right to get born healthy. Society has a right to have healthy future citizens.

In case the couple opts for some changes in their to-be-child, the woman has to constantly think about that change point determinately e.g. a couple with short stature wants a child with height not common in their clan or country, then the lady meditates on the lifestyle, garments, looks and likes of the Afghans (natives of Afghanisthan).

Panchabhautika composition of foetus:

Pruthvi	Jala	Agni / Teja	Vaayu	Aakaasha
Earth	Water	Fire	Gas	Atmosphere
Odour	Tongue	Beauty/form	Touch/tangibility	Hear/Sound
Sense of smell	Taste	Eyes	Sensation of	Auditory apparatus
Maintains	Cold	Sight/vision	touch	Lightness
calm	Softness	Light	Respiration	Minuteness/ fineness
Steadiness/	Stickiness	Digestion	process	Ability to pass from
stability	Wetness	Heat	Throbbing	small region
Heaviness	Blood	Bile/digestion	Lightness	Differentiation
Hardness	Semen	Temperature	Dryness	Different systems
Bones	Urine	Brain	Coarseness/	Lumens/space
Hair	Looseness	performance	roughness	
Nails	Fluids	Body skin	Initiate	
	Phlegm	colour	Carry nutrients	
	Fat	Aura/	and tissue	
	Muscles	brightness	elements	
		Valor	Activities/	
		Body growth	movements	

CHAPTER 2
Shreyasi Garbhasthaapanaa [Healthy conception]

Male has to continue use of Spermatogenic (*Shukra vruddhi sruti shudhdhi kara*) medicines along with observation of general rules of health mentioned earlier for getting a healthy child till pregnancy is confirmed.

Female has to continue observing general rules of health with specific rules to be followed during ovulation and copulation. In order to have a potent child with large limbs and eyes like a lion; a child full of valor, purity of mind and excellent genetic properties, the to-be-mother is given sweetened milk porridge (*kheera*) made from white barley, *ghee* and honey. The milk and *ghee* used should be of a white coloured cow having a white coloured alive healthy calf. The freshly made porridge is served in a silver or bronze vessel. This porridge is given twice a day for eight days from the day she takes purifying head-bath on completion of menstrual flow. Her clothes, linen, jewelry, colour of walls and curtains, food and drink should be clear white in colour. She tries to look at white colored articles like white bull, stallion and white sandal paste. She is entertained with stories according to her dream child.

The couple performs a *homa*. They sit west to the holy fire and south to the priest with the wife sitting left to her husband. They sit on a thick cloth in *Padmaasana*. They offer oblation in the fire and express their wish. The priest chants the holy hymns to that effect and blesses the couple accordingly. First the husband then the wife consumes remains of the sacrificial *ghee*.

A potent male, while following the rules of health, takes proper medicines to maintain quality and quantity of his sperms and vigour; observes the rules of copulation with an equally healthy, affectionate, pleased wife, in a pleasant environment, has better chances to conception.

Position, place, time and emotional status of the couple play an important role, hence importance of these rules from the day they dream to have a child. Cohabitation period is limited to eight days postmenstrual purification bath of the wife. They wear white comfortable dress and garlands of sweet fragrant flowers.

Friction of sexual organs during cohabitation produces heat which stimulates the local (*Apaana*) *vaayu*. This induces ejaculation of semen and ovum along with nutritive body fluids. When the spermatozoon and ovum get fertilized and remain confined to the uterus, *Aatma* (soul) along with *sookshma sharira* and *mana* enters the fertilized ovum. This imparts *Chetanaa* (life) to the cell mass. This is now termed *Garbha* (embryo).

Sadyogruhit Garbhaa Lakshana

(Signs observed immediately after copulation (before missing the first period) denoting fertilization and implantation):

These are signs felt by an alert female, immediately after *maithuna* (cohabitation) viz. she feels satisfied. She feels a throbbing sensation in the genitals. The semen is held back. A sense of fatigue, physical weakness, thirst, lassitude and loss of strength in the thighs is felt.

This is a waiting period. Hence requires continuation of the *Rutumati paricharyaa*.

To enhance quality of her child the to-be-mother is shown all auspicious signs e.g. take her to places of devotion, show her a water filled pot; she maintains pleasant mood, remains conscious about her child of dreams and continues observing the above stated health rules.

On missing her first period she is declared a carrying mother and is placed under prenatal care.

All texts of *Ayurveda* have advocated selection and medication for the desired sex in context of healthy and genitally potent (*Veeryavantm Sutam*) child. Since this humanitarian rule has been misused author has avoided discussing any such point. It will indeed be beneficial if the society comes out healthily and uses the Science for social betterment.

A short diagram to show the important elements involved in building, growth and development of a fetus:

Fetus is a fusion of *shudhdha* (healthy) *Aartava* (ovum) and *Shukra* (semen) in *Garbhaashaya* (healthy uterus) along with *Aatma, Mana, Prakriti, Vikaara, pancha Mahabhoota* (5basic elements), *pancha Tanmaatraa, pancha Gnaanendriya, pancha Karmendriya*; fusion of 24 basic elements takes form of zygote and ends into a complete human being.

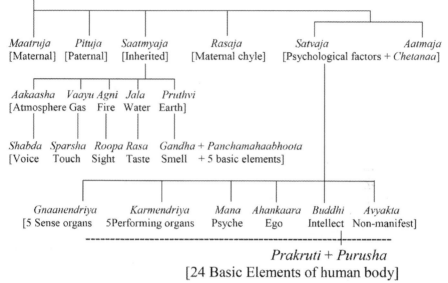

Shukra + Aartava + Jeevaatmaa = Garbha
[Semen + (Ovum + arterial blood in endometrium) + Consciousness = Fetus]

| Maatruja | Pituja | Saatmyaja | Rasaja | Satvaja | Aatmaja |
| [Maternal] | [Paternal] | [Inherited] | [Maternal chyle] | [Psychological factors + *Chetanaa*] | |

Aakaasha Vaayu Agni Jala Pruthvi
[Atmosphere Gas Fire Water Earth]

Shabda Sparsha Roopa Rasa Gandha + Panchamahaabhoota
[Voice Touch Sight Taste Smell + 5 basic elements]

Gnaanendriya Karmendriya Mana Ahankaara Buddhi Avyakta
[5 Sense organs 5Performing organs Psyche Ego Intellect Non-manifest]

Prakruti + Purusha
[24 Basic Elements of human body]

Importance of migratory soul: Vedic concept of birth and life after death is accepted by *Ayurveda*. All texts believe that in case of non-salvation after death, the Soul along with Psyche, Ego, Intellect, Non-manifested five basic elements, sense and performing organs (*sookshma sharira*) carries all its feelings and deeds of previous life as constitution of an embryo which bring about changes in likes, dislikes and feelings of a mother on completion of first trimester of pregnancy. This is said to affect structural and functional growth of the foetus. By following the safe road-map laid down by *Ayurveda*, a couple can bring about changes in status of the migratory soul.

Functions of balanced three *dosha*s in fetal development:

Vaayu (*Aakaasha* and *Vaayu*): divides the embryonic cells into limbs and organs

Pitta or *Teja dhaatu* (*Agni*): helps stimulate tissue metabolism

Kapha or *Ap dhaatu* (*Jala* and *Pruthvi*): maintains its liquid or semi-solid state needed for easy moldings and growth.

Functions of balanced *Panchamahaabhoota* in fetal development:

Aakaasha (space element): contributes to growth and development

Vaayu (gas element): divides cells into systems and body parts

Jala (water element): maintains semi-solid state, gives white colour to child

Teja (fire element): stimulates cell and tissue metabolism

Pruthvi (earth element): brings about compactness, gives black colour to child

Pruthvi and *Aakaasha*: Bluish black colour to child

Jala and *Aakaasha*: Bluish white colour to child

CHAPTER 3
Garbhini Paricharyaa [Prenatal care]

General instructions for to-be-mother:

"**Strong** human endeavor over-rules Luck."
Importance of *garbhini paricharyaa* (taking pre-natal care):
- Baby birth will be on maturity (no abortion or pre-mature delivery)
- Child will have senses and motor organs properly developed, placed and functioning
- Child is endowed with strength, complexion, intelligence and compactness
- There will be no difficulty during labour (chances of normal Labour are high)
- Physical, mental and emotional problems of the pregnant mother can be avoided
- A weak or deformed child becomes a source of constant burden and misery to parents and society hence importance of bringing a healthy potent child. A pregnant lady should be taken care of the way a pot filled up-to brim with oil is taken care while shifting it from one place to another: taking care the oil does not spill (*pooraimiva tailapaatramaasaiknnobhayataa antarvartane bhavatyupacharyaa*) because a slight oscillation or rough handling (stress, fatigue or excitement) causes spillage of oil which is similar to abortion or preterm birth in a pregnant lady.

Five factors responsible for healthy baby:
1) Excellence of semen and ovum
2) Purity of mind, thought and action of parents
3) Wholesomeness of maternal diet
4) Appropriate time, punctuality and regularity
5) Favourable environment, deeds and nature of parents and family

During its intra-uterine stay, fetus is dependent on mother for nutrition, respiration, responses, sleep etc. Fetal naval is attached through the umbilical cord and placenta to maternal uterus and thus to maternal blood circulation, heart and emotions.

Aahaara (Food):

During pregnancy, the end-product of digestion, chyle (*rasa dhaatu*) gets divided into three parts to accomplish three important functions, viz.:

1) Maternal nourishment,
2) Fetal nourishment and
3) Nourishment of breasts; to ensure timely and proper lactation.

The mother has to keep this in mind while planning her diet.

Take enough home-made fresh nutritive food dominant in sweet taste along with enough butter, *ghee*, milk and enough fluids.

Take rice cooked in sweetened milk (*kheera*) twice a day.

Give rice along with gruel of black gram (*Udad*) or decoction of radish (*Moolaa*) generously mixed with cow's *ghee*.

Avoid salty, sour, chilly, bitter, astringent or only sweet food (i.e. take a diet which is well balanced in all six tastes).

Avoid excessive, frequent or heavy to digest and dry type of food.

Avoid foods rich in pulses (they are heavy to digest).

Avoid taking very less quantity or food not having enough nourishment (may lead to emaciation or abortion).

Avoid foods having hot and sharp qualities e.g. spicy food, pickles (*aachaara*) wine, etc. may lead to bleeding and abortion.

Presently Recommended Dietary Allowances (R.D.A.) during pregnancy:

Food Nutrients	Required level to be taken
Energy	300 k cal. extra (2000 to 2100 k cal./day)
Protein	60 to 65 gms./day
Fat	30 gms./day
Calcium	1000 mgm./day
Iron	38 mgm./day
Folic acid	400 µgm./day
Ascorbic acid	60 mgm./day
Vitamin A	1000 I. U. /day

Maternal stomach produces less acid and pepsin hence she needs to be very careful for daily diet. Motility of maternal intestinal muscles gets reduced

which may lead to constipation. Hence easily digestible, liquid diet containing butter or *ghee* helps overcome this situation. Old rice cooked in milk is said to contain all the required nutrients and *Ayurveda* has advised the same.

Requirements generally differ from person to person, place of birth and stay, season to season and life style etc. factors.

Vyavahaara (Habits):

Advise her to continue with normal house-hold work which keeps her engaged.

Avoid excessive rest and sleep.

Avoid excessive laborious, annoying or exhaustive jobs.

Avoid too much walking or running with haste.

Avoid sitting or sleeping on hard, uneven surface or in strong, cold or hot wind.

Avoid sitting or sleeping in one position for a long time.

Avoid stress, being angry, critic, sorrowful, nervous, worrying or being jealous.

Avoid remaining hungry, thirsty or postponing natural calls.

Avoid sleeping during day or waking up late night, too much rest or sleep.

Avoid frequent bathing and frequent head baths.

An expectant mother should not start exercising, *praanayaama*, *yoga aasana*; take strong (avoidable) medicines, strong purgatives, go for *panchkarma* or blood-letting.

Avoid riding a bumpy vehicle or a bumpy road, travelling all alone or at night.

Avoid peeping into a well, looking at a valley, passing by a crematorium etc. places which create fear or sense of 'being unsafe'.

Paryaavarana (Environment):

Avoid hostile stressful atmosphere like beating, criticizing, horrifying, etc.

A child and mother friendly environment e.g. flowering plants, creepers, melodious music, heroic tales, friendly behaviour of husband, family and friends, in short an environment where she feels 'SAFE for herself and her child' is to be maintained.

Aushadha (Drugs):

Drugs that protect, help in proper implantation, growth, development and potency of the fetus are called *Garbha-sthaapaka*, *Prajaa-sthaapaka*, *Jeevaniya*, *Balya* drugs. These drugs are used as single or combination drugs with milk (*Ksheera*) or *Ghruta* (*ghee*) as vehicles through-out her prenatal, natal and postnatal periods (till she feeds the child i.e. about 2 years age) along with other special diets.

Smooth application (not massage) of warm oil over lower abdomen, pelvis, thighs, waist, sides, flank and back relives discomfort and eases uterine development.

Symptoms of pregnancy:

Advanced pregnancy is characterized by stoppage of menstruation, excessive salivation, dislike for food, aversion to good smell, sudden vomiting, anorexia, excessive desire for sour foods, relishes things not liked before, heaviness of limbs and eye-lids, deep pigmentation of lips and breast areola; slight pedal oedema, undue growth of hair and bulging of lower abdomen as time passes.

Antarvartani Paricharyaa (Care of the expectant mother: month by month):

[*Ayurveda* ante-natal care with fetal growth and development]

She has to observe all the rules for healthy life along with rules for to-be-mother specifically to enhance day to day and month to month development and growth of her fetus.

Prathama maasa (I month):
Foetal milestones:

Union of spermatozoon and ovum becomes well compounded (*sammurchchita*), all their elements get tinged (*sarva dhaatu kalushikruta*), jelly like appearance (at age 1 to 7 days), bubble shaped (at age 10 days), denser in consistency and shape of a muscle (at age 15-20 days), all five basic elements (*mahabhoota*) manifest themselves (at age 25 days) and foetus become conspicuous (no organs manifested) at the end of first month of life.

Aahaara (Food):

For the first ten days (*Sadya gruhita garbha*) ghee made from cow's milk (*go Ksheera*)along with drugs like *Prushniparni* (Uraria picta), *Kareera* (Capparis desidua), pure gold and silver, this *ghee* is given along with boiled water let to cool.

Sweetened cow's milk should be taken often.

She should take only that sweetened diet-she is used to in morning as well as evening, empty stomach.

Fresh *Aamla* (Emblica officinalis), *Shinghaada* (*Shrungataka*-Trapa bispinosa) and other seasonal fruits, vegetables like *Dudhi* (Bottle gourd), *Paalaka* (Spinacia oleracea), *Surana* (Corm of Amorphophallus campanulatus Blume.) are to be used judiciously

Aushadha (Drugs):

Ayurveda has not advised any medicines; only fetal friendly drugs are used as prophylactics e.g. *Yashtimadhu* (Glycyrrhiza glabra Linn.), *Parushaka* (Grewia asiatica) with home-made butter, etc.

Take milk prepared with sweet medicines.

Take *Apaamarga* (Achyranthes aspera Linn) and *Sahachara* (Nilgirianthus ciliatus / Barleria ciliate Roxb.) boiled in cow's milk.

Take lotus seeds (cover and inner green shoot removed) as per requirement.

The woman should roast *Shaali* (a type of rice) rice and inhale its fumes. This rice should be soaked in water for some time. This mixture is sieved and the woman herself instills this mixture in her right nostril with help of sterile cotton wool. That portion which reaches the mouth is swallowed. This process is for vitalizing and firm anchoring of the fetus.

Dveetiya maasa (II month):
(**Vyakta garbha avasthaa**):
Foetal milestones:

The cell mass hardens to take the shape of a tumour (*granthi*), elongated or oval shape (*peshi*) or semi-circle or hemispherical shape (*arbuda*). The shape denotes its future sexual development viz. *granthi* shaped embryo develops into a male, *peshi* into a female and *arbuda* into a hermaphrodite or an individual lacking clear sexuality; at age of 50 days buds of appendages start sprouting.

Aahaara (Food): (advised):

Take cow's milk with *Yashtimadhu* (Glycyrrhiza glabra Linn.).

Take food mixed with *Kaakoli* (Roscoea procera wall.) or *Ashwagandhaa* (Withania somnifera Dunal) and sugar.

Take food made from *Yava* (Barley; Hordeum vulgare), *Shaali* type rice, wheat, green gram, red gram, jaggery, sugar, *Sindhava* (rock salt) salt; fruits—banana, berries, coconut, jackfruit

Take *Kheera* (rice cooked in milk and sweetened), infrequent *Dudhi* (Bottle gourd) *halvaa* [not made from dried milk (*maavaa*)].

Make frequent use of milk, butter, *ghee* (made from butter) and honey.

Paryaavarana (Environment):

Remain aloof from anything that tires the body and disturbs the mind.

Aushadha (Drugs):
Sweet (*Madhura*) group of drugs with milk
Kaakoli group of drugs (given in appendix) with milk
Jeevaniya group of drugs (given in appendix) along with *ghee*, milk
Lotus (Nelumbo nucifera) seeds

Trutiya maasa (III month):
Foetal milestones:

All sense organs, all the limbs emerge simultaneously in the form of projections, due to manifestation of action of the sense organs and the latent mind, fetal throbbing and cardiac activity are noted. Foetus is said to remember its past life actions and depending upon them feels happy or sorrowful.

Aahaara (Food):
Take cow's milk with honey and cow's *ghee*.
Take sweetened cow's milk.
Take sweetened liquid diet.
Take *Shashthi* rice cooked in milk (*Kheera*).
Take *Krusharaa* [*khichdi* (rice and pulses in a proper combination cooked with 16 times water)].
Take food prepared from *Kodri* (Paspalum scrobiculatum aka Kodo millet), *Masoor* (orange dal), *Chanaa* (gram), *Kulthi* (Dolichos biflorus Linn.; Horse gram), *Raaja-maasha* (black gram), *Beeda lavana* (a type of salt) added to taste.
Avoid use of buffalo's milk, curd or *ghee*.
Avoid using *Kolu* (*Kushmaanda*; Benincasa hispida Thunb. Cogn; Winter melon), *Vans ankur* (bamboo shoot).

Vyavahaara (Habits):
Avoid day sleeping, applying *kaajal* or medicines to bring tears.
Avoid crying, frequent bathing, excessive skin care, massaging, nail biting, travelling, staying alone or going to unknown places.
Avoid walking with speed, running or laughing loudly.

Paryaavarana (Environment):
Follow as per previous months.

Aushadha (Drugs): Follow as per previous months.

Thus completes the first trimester (three months) of pregnancy.

Chaturtha maasa [mother is called *Dauhridini*-one who has two hearts] (IV month and II Trimester):

Foetal milestones:
Foetus stabilizes, heart is endowed with consciousness, organic differentiation becomes clear, sense organs develop, physical and mental activities manifest, foetus remembers happenings in past life, lanugo starts growing, mother starts gaining weight, mother reflects the desires of her fetus and longs for varied things like food, clothes, ornaments etc. Scientific fulfillment of these wishes is said to be helpful for future fetal growth and development. These wishes also predict possible qualities of the unborn.

Sr. No.	Longings of *Dauhridini*	Possible qualities of to-be-child
1	Desire to see the King	Child will be rich and will hold high positions in life
2	Desire for fine clothes, ornaments, etc.	Child will be beautiful with aesthetic taste
3	Desire to visit hermitage	Child will be self-controlled
4	Desire to see divine idol or auspicious image	Child will grace an august assembly
5	Desire to see a wild animal	Child will be of cruel and wild temperament
6	Desire to take beef	Child will be strong, vigorous, capable of sustaining fatigue or physical pain
7	Desire for buffalo's meat	Child will be hairy, valiant and with eyes having red colour
8	Desire for boar's meat	Child will be valiant but sleepy
9	Desire for flesh of a particular animal	Child will develop similar traits of character in life peculiar to that animal

Aahaara (Food):
Use cow's milk and milk butter abundantly.
Use cow's milk and *ghee* with honey.
Use *Shaali, Shashthika* rice regularly with curd made from cow's milk.

Fruits—sweet-sour grapes fresh or dried.

Food she likes, that are palatable and contain sour taste.

Vyavahaara (Habits):

Non fulfillment of special desires (*dauhruda*) may lead to congenital abnormalities like disfigure, abnormalities in arms, legs, eyes, having short stature, less intelligence, etc.

Paryaavarana (Environment):

Follow as per previous months.

Aushadha (Drugs):

Aindri (Citrullus colocynthis), *Brahmi* (Bacopa monnieri), *Shataavari* (Asparagus racemosus), *Durvaa* (Cynodon dactylon), *Shivaa* (Terminalia chebula), *Yashtimadhu* (Glycyrrhiza glabra), *Padmaka* (Nelumbo nucifera), *Utpala* (Nymphaea alba), *Udumbara* (Ficus racemosa), *Balaa* (Sida cordifolia), *Ati balaa* (Abutilon indicum), *Saarivaa* (Roots of Hemidesmus indicus), *Anantaa* (Hemidesmus indicus), *Devdaaru* (Cedrus deodara), *Prushniparni* (Uraria picta) etc. child friendly, growth and development enhancing drugs should be used abundantly as single or in combination, in powder form, with cow's milk, boiled in cow's milk (*Ksheera paaka*) or with cow's *ghee* under expert medical supervision.

Panchama maasa (V month):
Foetal milestones:

Enhancement of muscle tissues and blood, mind functions manifest (*Mana abhivyakti*), mother becomes emaciated.

Aahaara (Food):

Ghee made from milk

Shashthi rice cooked in cow's milk to make *Paayasa*, *Doodhapaaka* (rice boiled in 16 times milk so that it contains more of milk part).

Take food rich in milk, *ghee* and sugar crystals.

Take *yavaagu* (light gruel prepared out of rice, water and mild spices) prepared in milk.

Take cow's milk with honey and cow's *ghee*.

Vyavahaara (Habits):

Follow as per previous months.

Paryaavarana (Environment):
  Mother is tied *Rakshaa* (Charm).

Aushadha (Drugs): Follow as per previous months.

Shashthama maasa (VI month):
Foetal milestones:
  Increase in strength and complexion, tendons, vessels, lanugo, hair, nails and bones start to appear, intellectual development occurs (*budhdhi vyakti*), mother feels loss in strength and complexion.

Aahaara (Food):
  Sweetened curd made from cow's milk.
  Use food which is rich in cow's *ghee* and sugar.
  Cow's milk and *ghee* with sweet group of medicines like *Yashtimadhu*.

Vyavahaara (Habits):
  Follow as per previous months.

Paryaavarana (Environment):
  Follow as per previous months.

Aushadha (Drugs):
  Give cow's *ghee* with *Gokharu* (Tribulus terrestris) powder.
  Yavaagu prepared with *Gokharu* (Tribulus terrestris) powder.

  Thus completes the Second trimester (three months) of pregnancy.

Saptama maasa (VII month and III trimester):
  Breasts begin developing in embryo at around its six weeks of intra-uterine life. This development continues till birth when the milk ducts are fully developed. In a female baby, further development takes place during adolescence when they gradually enlarge to take form of adult breasts which contain milk glands, ducts, supportive connective tissue and protective fatty tissue.
  During this last phase of pregnancy, the maternal breasts are in their active phase preparing for lactation post-delivery hence they need more attention. The breasts are cleaned gently with warm water. Both nipples are

cleaned with cotton soaked in warm water and dried. Sesame oil is applied gently to maintain their smoothness and softness.

Foetal milestones:
Wholesome growth (*sarvaavayava paripoornataa*) hence mother feels restless and tired.

Aahaara (Food):
Use food rich in cow's *ghee* and sugar which promote healthy fetal growth and development.
Use cow's milk with cow's *ghee* and *Yashtimadhu* (Glycyrrhiza glabra).
Less sweet and less liquid content in diet is given.

Vyavahaara (Habits):
Different oils, decoctions are applied softly over her abdomen specifically lower part with strokes going upwards i.e. towards naval from all sides.

Paryaavarana (Environment):
Follow as per previous months.

Aushadha (Drugs):
Cow's milk and *ghee* prepared with *Prushniparni* (Uraria picta), *Shaaliparni* (Desmodium gangeticum) etc. drugs.
Cow's milk and *ghee* prepared with sweet group (*madhura gana*) of drugs.

Ashtama maasa (VIII month):
Foetal milestones:
Essence of all tissues which gives physical and mental strength, *Oja* becomes unsteady (*a-sthiri bhavati Oja*) this brings about unsteadiness in maternal behaviour i.e. she suddenly feels cheerful and suddenly gets sorrowful. If *Oja* gets vitiated, it causes serious diseases and may lead to death of mother or baby, hence birth is avoided.

Aahaara (Food):
Yavaagu prepared in cow's milk is given with *ghee*.
Ghevar (a sweet dish) is specifically given during this month.
Avoid cold, spicy, preserved, and heavy to digest food; food having bitter or astringent taste.
Avoid vices like strong coffee, frequent tea, alcohol, etc.

Vyavahaara (Habits):

Cravings of the lady are satisfied to help her beget a child bearing good look, character, valor and intelligence.

Paryaavarana (Environment):

Follow as per previous months.

Seemantonnayana Samsakaara is performed in case of primi gravida.

Mangala karma (ritual) is performed.

Aushadha (Drugs):

Sneha basti (medicated oil enema) is given to control *vaayu* and avoid constipation. It lubricates and eases tissues of the anal canal.

Navama maasa (IX month):

Foetal milestones:

Foetus completes its physical, sensory and mental development (*paripoornataa*). It is like a ripe fruit ready to get detached from its twig.

Aahaara (Food):

Take boiled rice mixed with sesame oil or *ghee*.

Give *Yavaagu* with sesame oil or *ghee*.

Give different types of family or local food to acquaint the baby with them.

Give food as per mother's choice taking care of the fetus.

Vyavahaara (Habits):

Follow as per previous months.

Paryaavarana (Environment):

Follow as per previous months.

Start prepare mother (both physically and mentally) for Labour.

On an auspicious day and constellation she is admitted to a *Prasootaagaara* specially prepared room adjacent to labour room; irrespective of her pains and fetal status.

The room is comfortable, friendly and free of cold, humidity, animals, insects, microbes;

contains all necessary equipments, medicines, emergency care appliances, drugs, experienced attendants, experienced maids, experienced *Vaidya*, experienced *Kaumaarabhrutya* (expert in neonatology), *Kumaaraadhaara* (neonate caretaker), telephone, call bell, etc.

Aushadha (Drugs and *Karma*):

Sneha basti (medicated oil enema) is administered to maintain balance of *vaayu*.

Yoni sneha pichchu (medicated oil vaginal tampon) maintains suppleness and elasticity.

All necessary medicines needed to maintain health of the *antarvartani* are given with due care for fetal wellness and onset of labour.

A pregnant woman consciously stays away from anything that can harm her and her baby.

From X month till labour:

Normally labour takes place during the ninth or tenth month; rarely does it occur in the eleventh or twelfth month. Labour beyond the twelfth month and before the ninth month is abnormal.

Normal fetal position in maternal womb is head low, facing mother with folded limbs (*aabhugna abhi-mukhaha shete garbho garbhaashaye striyaaha*).

It gets born with head coming first.

While performing any *karma* (operations) strict aseptic precautions are mandatory. Oil, *ghee, yoni prakshaalana* (douche) or *basti* material, etc. are always kept for individual use. *Ayurveda* has its own way of aseptic practice which is very strict and rarely practiced.

Aahaara (Food):

Avoid excessive spicy, chilled, hot, heavy to digest food, preserved; dry, hard, having changed taste and foul smell.

Avoid taking excessive nutritive or excessive low calorie diet.

Avoid keeping fasts, staying hungry or thirsty.

Avoid taking food of one taste.

Avoid over eating, eating when the previous food is not digested.

Avoid drinking chilled water or drinks, shakes, etc.

In short observe all the previously stated food rules.

Vyavahaara (Habits):

Continue with abstinence.

Avoid staying alone.

Avoid excessive exercise, *bhastrika* etc. tough types of *praanayaama*.

Try and concentrate only on the fetal growth, development and needs.

Keep body, clothes, thoughts and wishes clean and clear.

Avoid using tobacco, wine, drugs etc.

Offer prayers regularly, maintain faith and avoid disrespecting anybody.

For those who cannot afford staying in the special room under constant expert observation: are away from family and cannot stay away from work:

Avoid excessive running or walking with haste.

Avoid excessive stress or exposure to strong emotional upsets like flaring up, gripping fear, and excessive sorrow.

Avoid bearing heavy loads or bending down so that abdomen is pressurized.

Avoid hard work duties or traveling on an uncomfortable road or in an uncomfortable vehicle i.e. avoid all that is injurious to the sense and working organs.

Avoid wearing tight clothes or tying a tight thread or band on any part of the body.

Avoid sleeping during day or staying awake till late night.

Avoid sitting or sleeping uncomfortably, on hard uneven surface, in a wrong posture or wearing a thick heavy clothes or blanket.

Avoid postponing natural urges or not attending them properly.

Avoid staying in strong wind, scorching sun or severe exposure to heat or cold.

Avoid sitting on very tall, high, uncomfortable chair.

There is only one target to be achieved and that is "Child of Dreams".

Paryaavarana (Environment):

Avoid looking at or coming into close contact with fearful or abnormal looking people, stories, sculptures or paintings.

Avoid staying in an uncomfortable and hostile environment like strong or offensive odors, empty houses, near crematorium, peeping or going into wells, deep holes, digging, excavations, shelling trees or plants etc. destructive activities.

Avoid an environment that angers; is fearful or creates sense of unsafely

Aushadha (Drugs):

Avoid body purification like *panchkarma*.

Avoid applying oil, massaging, bloodletting, applying medicated powders for beautification, remaining in tub for a long time, taking sauna bath, etc.

Avoid taking strong medicines like purgatives.

Avoid procedures that cause excessive sweating and *kshaara karma* etc. avoidable surgeries.

Fetus when provided a favourable atmosphere, grows, develops and matures well in the uterus failing which leads to various pathologies or morbidity.

Some of the reasons for fetal pathology are:
- Defects in spermatozoa or ovum or both.
- Defects in the female genitalia specially uterus, adnexa and *Apaana vaayu.*
- Performing coitus at wrong time, in wrong position at wrong place.
- Mis-deeds of previous life of the incarnating soul.
- Defects in the diet, behaviour, thoughts and deeds of the parents specially the to-be-mother.
- Result of sinful acts of the parents in this or previous life.
- Various illnesses of mother especially contagious or chronic illnesses and genital infections.

General maternal milestones of healthy pregnancy:

Sr. No.	Milestones	Duration of pregnancy
1	Positive Urine Test	4-6 weeks
2	Amenorrhoea	4 to 40 weeks
3	Morning sickness	4 to 14 weeks
4	Breast changes	6 to 40 weeks
5	Bladder symptoms	6 to 14 weeks
		36 to 40 weeks
6	Cervical changes	6 to 40 weeks
7	Fetal changes noted in Sonography	6 weeks onwards
8	Palpable uterine changes	7 weeks onwards
9	Vaginal and Vulval changes	8 to 40 weeks
10	Hegar's sign Positive	8 to 40 weeks
11	Uterus palpable per abdomen	10 weeks onwards
12	Ballottement	14 to 32 weeks
13	X ray visibility of fetus	14 weeks onwards
14	Quickening: in Multi gravida/Para	16 to 40 weeks
14 A	Quickening: in Primi gravida	18 to 40 weeks
15	Increasing maternal abdominal girth	16 weeks onwards
16	Palpable uterine contractions	20 weeks onwards
17	Palpable fetal movements	20 weeks onwards
18	Audible fetal heart sound	24 weeks onwards
19	Palpable fetal parts	26 weeks onwards

Guideline to week-wise growth of fetus:

I Trimester: (First 3 months of intra-uterine life)	
Week 1	The week after the last menstruation. Ovulation may occur.
Week 2	Most fertile period of cycle. Perfect time to get pregnant.
Week 3	On successful copulation, fertilization takes place. Haploid cells become diploid on fusion. Fertilized ovum reaches the uterine cavity.
Week 4	Blastocyst (cluster of cells) gets embedded in uterine wall (Endometrium). Placental group of cells get differentiated and start to separate from fetal cells.
Week 5	Embryo length 3 cms. Early Neural tube (which will develop into brain and spinal cord) formed. Correct Urine for pregnancy test result can be obtained 12 days after conception.
Week 6	Embryo looks like a "Coma". Cells of heart, liver, musculo-skeletal system is established.
Week 7	Limb buds are formed. Arms more advanced than legs.
Week 8	Facial structure is formed. Head is disproportionately large. Both jaws, eyes and ears are present. Generally first U. S. G. is done.
Week 9	Tiny hands and feet start to grow. Heart beats are strong enough to be detected on Ultrasound scan.
Week 10	Wrists, elbows, hips and knees give flexibility. Internal organs start to manifest.
Week 11	Fetal movements start. Umbilical cord gets coiled: most often in anti-clock direction.
Week 12	Digestive system is ready to absorb glucose. Placenta starts providing nourishment and carry away waste products.
II Trimester: (Second 3 months of intra-uterine life)	
Week 13	Baby curled up with legs crossed and arms placed in front over face. Tiny toes get separated. Ankle joint mobility allows it to kick. Body size about mother's closed fist.
Week 14	Head rounded neck longer, hands more usable, ear folds forming, all body parts forming and start differentiating. It is able to differentiate the foods mother eats. This affects its taste sense in later life.
Week 15	Grows at a rapid pace. Skin is thin and transparent. Eyelids closed with noticeable eye-lashes.

Week 16	Bones mature (increased demand for calcium); heartbeats can be heard-baby listens mother's heartbeats; immune system develops; baby starts making antibodies; hears mother's voice: perfect time to start active interaction: helps designing baby's nature and sociability. Mother listening to own heart beat and keeping it slow and steady relaxes the baby. Anxious mother with increased heart rate startles her baby and disturbs its nervous development.
Week 17	Fat starts depositing under skin; heart pumps up-to 24 liters blood/day.
Week 18	Hands and feet develop. Unique toe and finger-print starts to form. Urine and bowel system start processing.
Week 19	Skin is covered with hair to help regulate body temperature. Vernix (greasy substance) forms over the skin to form a water-proof barrier against amniotic fluid.
Week 20	Second U. S. G. done to ensure proper development of baby and placental position. Soft and gentle touch over abdomen establishes emotions rapport.
Week 21	Sense of taste and touch are developed. Heart gets stronger. Gets control over own movements.
Week 22	Brain develops rapidly. It has patterns of sleep and wakefulness which may not coincide with those of its mother.
Week 23	Gets hiccups, may swallow amniotic fluid. Mother feels punches and kicks clearly as they are stronger.
Week 24	Lungs grow, breathing patterns established. Hearing well developed so it can appreciate music. Perfect time for Papa to get close and personal with his baby.
III Trimester: (Third and last 3 months of intra-uterine life)	
Week 25	Insulating fat starts depositing. Yawns a lot to unblock fluid from ears. Nostrils start to open. Time to play music mother enjoys (appreciates same music post-birth) avoiding shrill harsh high pitch sounds.
Week 26	Deposited fat gives due shape to organs e.g. chubby cheeks. finger nails, eyelashes and eyebrows are visible. Torch or any shining light over abdomen startles the baby.
Week 27	Pulls faces, sticks out tongue, sucks thumb, etc. activities become clear
Week 28	Lungs develop enough to breathe (if born). Eyelids open though vision capacity is not well established.

Week 29	Sleeps a lot. Rapid eye movements are noted: sign that it might be dreaming.
Week 30	Hearing well developed. Startles on exposure to loud sounds. Grasps hands together: helps in its nervine development.
Week 31	Hair starts to wear off. Looks more like a human baby.
Week 32	Makes vigorous movements. If born, can hear, smell, taste, see and feel touch.
Week 33	Rolls from side to side coinciding maternal position.
Week 34	Enzymes needed for food digestion commence.
Week 35	Developed to cover all available uterine space: baby cannot move freely.
Week 36	Recognizes mother's voice. Generally takes vertex position. If still in breech position, there is still time to change.
Week 37	Getting ready to be born. When awake, practices on sucking reflex.
Week 38	Since available space keeps shrinking, movements get more difficult. Puts on weight which helps balance temperature after birth.
Week 39 and 40	Fully developed and ready for a healthy living in extra-uterine atmosphere.

Even if birth does not take place, nothing to worry.
A properly nourished healthy baby gets born between 38 to 42 weeks of intra-uterine life.

Pregnancy & birth, May 2012, Pg. 98 to 100, askmum.co.uk.com

Practical Parenting & Pregnancy, January 2012, Pg. 37, madeformums.com

CHAPTER 4

Prasootaa paricharyaa [Natal care]

From the time of completion of third trimester of pregnancy to completion of third stage of labour, series of events take place in the whole maternal body especially genitals. Labour is an effort to expel the viable products of conception out of the uterus through the vagina into the outer world. This complex process is called *Prasava* in *Ayurveda*.

Delivery and labour are not synonyms. Expulsion or extraction of a viable foetus out of the uterus can take place without labour as in Cesarean Section.

Normal labour is spontaneous in onset and occurs at term. The baby is in vertex i.e. mid-head coming first and takes place without un-due prolongation. It ends with minimum or no aids and without any complications to mother and child.

Importance of time of onset of labour:

Though the baby is able to survive in the outer world on completion of six months of intra-uterine life; it is not Ripe. As a ripe fruit gets detached by itself when its twig gets ripe symbolizes a fetus getting detached from its attachment to mother, on attaining maturity, is an appropriate metaphor used in the texts of *Ayurveda*. As unripe fruit detached before time does not have proper taste, smell and nutritive properties, so is seen in a pre-term (pre-mature) baby. According to *Ayurveda* the normal period of birth is from completion of 9 months to 12 months of intra-uterine life. [Google news of 7 August 2013: Fetus can stay up-to 5 weeks beyond the normal 9 months intra-uterine stay and is normal. Fetuses behave variedly.]

Time of entering the *Prasootaagaara* (Ante labour room):

Ayurveda believes that a lady should be kept aloof from the external and social environment to help her stabilize herself and have active relations with her baby. She is not brought to the labour room.

Thus on completion of the eight month of pregnancy, she is ceremoniously entered to the *Prasootaagaara* on an auspicious day and constellation, irrespective of onset of pains.

A cow, pious elderly person, fire in a pot and a pot full of water go ahead of her to ensure an auspicious atmosphere. She enters the room or place with her right leg first which energizes her *Surya naadi*. Sun is not merely a source of heat and energy according to *Hindu* culture. The *Surya naadi* is very important in all matters of health, self-confidence, positivity of thought and good fortune.

Society needs to understand importance of duties before rights.

A perfect human will always fulfill his duties even when they are not made known.

Signs of onset of labour:

Labour is said to have set when severe pains are felt in lower abdomen spreading towards back, lumber region and thighs. Though these pains will bear down the woman; as labour progresses, she feels lightness over heart (*mukte hrudaya bandhane*). With each passing hour and as labour progresses, her abdomen remains toned for a longer duration. She may feel urges to void stool. Frequent urge to void urine denotes progress of labour. Passage of sticky thick mucus through vagina denotes expansion of internal cervical orifice (progress of labour which should be felt along with pain and heaviness in thighs; *s-shoola jaghane naari gneyaa saa tu prajaayini*).

Moment the lady starts feeling any of these signs, attendant is supposed to call on the *Vaidya*.

All further steps are to be handled by an expert Midwife Only.

All *Ayurveda* texts have talked of Institutional delivery only.

Prasootaagaara [*Prasuti bhavana*: of which Labour room is only a part]

- The ground selected should be free of boulders, bones and such inauspicious things.

- Building should be made under supervision of *Vaastu* expert. Building should be on an elevated ground or base so that it keeps off dampness, dirt, insects and unwanted intruders like mosquitoes, flies, snakes, scorpions etc.

- Building should be constructed in the east or north portion of the plot. The main door of the building should face East or North.

- Building should be made from wood [*Bilva* (Aegle marmelos), *Tinduka* (Diospyros malabarica aka The Gaub Tree), *Inguda* (Balanites roxburghii), *Bhallaataka* (Semecarpus anacardium Linn), *Varuna* (Crataeva Nurvala) or *Khadira* (Acacia catechu)]. In ancient days each woman was delivered in a specially made Labour cottage befitting her needs. On completion of *Sootikaa kaala* (post-natal period) and *Nava jaata kaala* (neonatal period i.e. initial 45 days), the cottage was destroyed. This concept is indeed very hygienic but in the present scenario, not many can afford it hence the point is not elaborated. It is known that wood maintains temperature and protects from humidity; much needed for both mother and child.

- It should have properly planned places for fire, water, pestle etc.

- It should be comfortable in all seasons.

- It should contain all necessary instruments, appliances, medicines, drugs, clothing, linen etc. properly placed.
  (Diagram given)

- Its staff should be experienced, good mannered, well behaved. Staff should have children with good health. The women should be vigilant, decisive, have feelings for children and of hard working nature. The staff should also contain old aged, knowledgeable people including women expert in conducting normal labour and handling (taking care of) neonate.

Diagram of a *Prasuti bhavana* (Obstetric care unit):

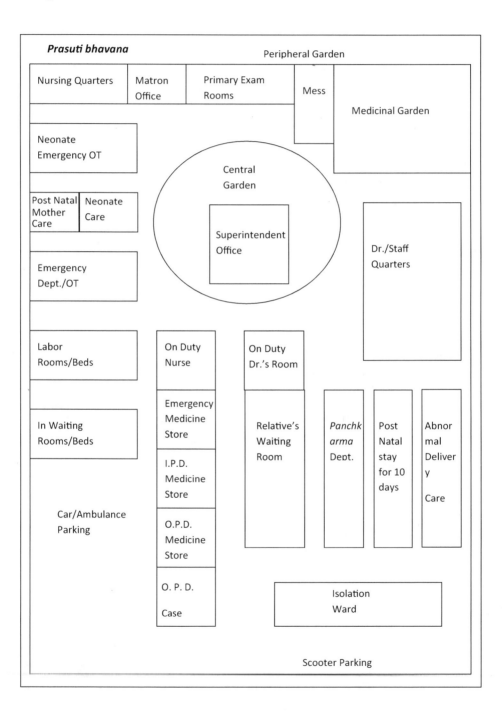

Prasuti bhavana

Peripheral Garden

Nursing Quarters

Matron Office

Primary Exam Rooms

Mess

Medicinal Garden

Neonate Emergency OT

Central Garden

Post Natal Mother Care

Neonate Care

Superintendent Office

Dr./Staff Quarters

Emergency Dept./OT

Labor Rooms/Beds

On Duty Nurse

On Duty Dr.'s Room

In Waiting Rooms/Beds

Emergency Medicine Store

Relative's Waiting Room

Panchkarma Dept.

Post Natal stay for 10 days

Abnormal Delivery Care

I.P.D. Medicine Store

Car/Ambulance Parking

O.P.D. Medicine Store

O. P. D. Case

Isolation Ward

Scooter Parking

Kumaaraagaara (Well Baby Clinic):

- It should be made under directions of *vaastuvidyaa kushala* (architect)

- It should be appropriate, good looking and comfortable.

- It should be protected from entry of strong wind and strong sunlight.

- It should be well protected from canines, rodents, flies and microbes.

- It should contain different sections for water, *ulukhala* (pestle), toilets, baths and kitchen. In short it should be comfortable in every aspect and season e.g. there should be seasonal provisions for sitting and sleeping arrangements, neonate and baby care, etc.

- It should be kept well protected from all types of infections by *bali, mangala, homa, shuchi* (cleanliness), *praayashchitta* (asking for pardon), etc. rituals.

- Staff: Senior, experienced, dedicated and hardworking.

- Linen, bedding, blankets etc. should be soft, made from friendly yarn and colour, clean, well fumigated (with child friendly fumes) using *Yava* (Hordeum vulgare Linn), *Sarshapa* (Brassia nigra), *Atasi* (Linum usitatissium), *Hingu* (Ferula narthex), *Guggulu* (Combiphora mukul), *Vachaa* (Acorus calamus), *Choraka* (Angelica glauca), *Vayasthaa* (Terminalia chebula), *Palankasha* (Ficus locor), etc. with cow's *ghee* and dung.

- Care taken for proper and total disposal of feces, urine, soiled clothes, etc.

- All clothes should be properly washed, dried in direct sunlight and properly fumigated before re-use.

- The child is adorned with precious stones and *Aindri* (Citrullus colocynthia), *Gunjaa* (Abrus precatorius), etc. drugs as per advice of experienced *Atharva-veda-aachaarya* (expert in the science of immunity).

- It contains various types of toys that are light weighed, have various shapes resembling birds, domestic animals, common house hold appliances, etc.; have melodious tunes; but should never have sharp edges or points or harmful colours such that they can injure the child while handling or playing; or create fear in its mind.

- A child should never be frightened. A child should never be called by frightful, inauspicious names like *Raakshasa*, *Pishaacha*, *Putanaa*, etc. names.

- Infected people should not enter (a social disciple needs to be framed) the *Kumaaraagaara*. If by any chance the child gets infected, the infection is immediately brought under control by proper measures, medicines and treatment using low power, child friendly, easy to digest drugs having sweet agreeable taste. There are ample of non-toxic, non-steroidal emergency drugs in *Ayurveda*.

- Thus a child is looked after from birth till it gains enough strength to get socialized i.e. about six month age.

Diagram of *Kumaaraagaara*:

(Neo-natal & Paediatric O.P.D., O.T., Ward, Day care centre, Special care centre)

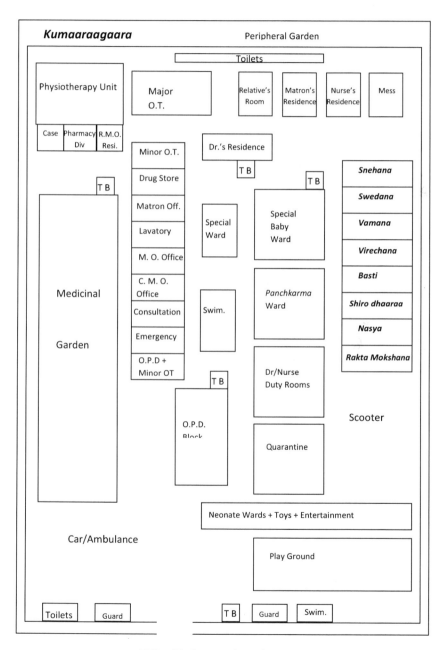

T.B.=Toilets and Bathrooms

CHAPTER 5
Sootikaa paricharyaa [Post-natal care of mother]

Sootikaa is defined as a lady in labour, who has expelled placenta (*prasoota api n sootaa stri aparaa chet na nirgataa*).

Importance of *Sootikaa paricharyaa* (observing special rules):

The woman passes through a very delicate phase during the post-labour period (immediate post-delivery to first six weeks or re-commencement of menstruation period). Hence *Ayurveda* advocates special care and precautions regarding diet and day to day intensive monitoring (*Sootikaa paricharyaa*). She has to take care of herself, her genitals, lactation and up-bringing the neo-nate. This holds extra importance in primi-para, twin delivery or assisted delivery cases.

The worn out mother who is not taken care of or herself avoids the said rules, faces grave problems or irreversible complications (*sootikaa vyaadhi*) which may lead her to permanent disability, disease, infertility or even death.

Food taken by a pregnant lady gets divided in-to three parts:

A portion nourishes the mother, second part the growing foetus and third part nourishes maternal breasts preparing them for lactation. At end of Labour baby gets born and placenta is expelled. This phenomenon occurs due to activation of *Apaana vaayu*. The same *vaayu* secretes lochia. Contraction of uterus, ligaments etc. and stimulation of lactation takes place in a matter of hours. This speed has to be maintained in order to bring the lady back to routine in a very short prescribed time-span.

Sootikaa paricharyaa is a routine total care of neo-mother. She is given whole body massage, typical bath, and nutritive liquid easy to digest diets befitting her body needs, prevalent season and baby requirements.

During initial six months of life, the baby is totally dependent on maternal milk. Maternal food, thoughts and behaviour; physical, mental and emotional factors directly affect the quality and quantity of lactation which in turn affect the physical, mental and emotional health and development of the child.

The initial breast milk is a clear sticky liquid known as colostrum (*Piyusha* in *Ayurveda*). This gradually changes through the transitional phase to fully mature milk during the initial fifteen days of baby. This is nature's boon. Baby is provided with food that is easily accepted and digested with all the required nutrition.

Method of breast feeding:

Mother prepares herself for feeding. This is done by drinking a large quantity of fluid type food and boiled water. She cleans her breasts specially the nipples. Coaxes her baby (as in pre-coital play which stimulates both partners), talks with it and then sits upright.

The position of mother and baby should be comfortable to both yet there are rules regarding their position which need to be followed for betterment of both.

Mother needs to remain relaxed and free for her baby so as to properly feed and nurture it. The initial days are vital for their relationship. The more they stay to-gather, the earlier a healthy relationship gets established. The best way is to assist them only when needed.

Mother takes baby in her arms so that head remains at a higher level from body, it can suck without effort and a space is left between baby's lips and breasts so that the baby is able to breathe with ease while sucking at the nipple. This avoids air ingestion also.

Never pull the breasts from baby's mouth. Mother should smoothly introduce her clean index finger from side, into the baby's mouth and slowly withdraw her nipple.

In a satisfied baby, this manoevre is never needed. The baby leaves the nipple the moment it is satisfied and that is actually the way a baby needs to be fed.

Never avoid a night feed demand.

On completion of feed, in case there is residue feed, she removes it manually or an expert assists her in draining the residual milk manually. When both the breasts are relaxed, she washes them with warm water, taking special care of nipples. She dries the breasts and nipples with clean, fumigated, cotton cloth. She then applies warm *ghee* delicately over both the nipples.

Avoid wearing bra or any tight fitting dress over breasts during breast-feeding phase.

Signs and symptoms of vitiation of breast milk:

Maternal lactation (*Stanya*) gets vitiated with the three *dosha* (*Vaata*, *Pitta* and *Kapha*).

Vitiated maternal milk causes different discomforts and diseases to the baby e.g. constipation or diarrhoea, colour of urine is white or yellow, urine is high in density, *jwara* (fever), *arochaka* (anorexia), *trushnaa* (thirst), *chardi* (vomiting), *vijrumbhana* (yawning), *anga vikshepa* (twisting), *apasmaara* (convulsions), *bhrama* (vertigo), *vepathu* (trembling), *koojana* (making typical uncomfortable sound specially during sleep), inflammation of ear, eye or mucous membrane of mouth.

So long a mother willfully breast-feeds her baby with love; there is generally no difficulty in feeding or even prolonged feeding.

Generally problems are encountered when:

Infant causes	Maternal causes
Premature / weak baby	Breast engorgement / Mastitis / Breast abscess
Assisted / prolonged / difficult Labour	Sore / painful nipples
Cleft lip / palate	Fissured / cracked nipples
Mentally retarded	Blocked ducts
Twins etc. multiple births	Not taking enough water / liquids
Improper management of neonate	Difficult / assisted Labour
After crying for long time	Post Caesarean section
Congenital infections	Infections
Illness e.g. fever, convulsions	Illness e.g. fever, diarrhoea, vomiting, etc.

Benefits of breast feeding:

Benefits to infant	Benefits to mother
Better chance for survival	Feeling of achievement: Satisfaction
Immunity is maintained	Fulfillment of motherhood
Easily digested	Stimulates passing of lotia
Premature babies thrive easily	Stimulates involution of uterus
Does not cause allergies	-
Protects against arteriosclerotic diseases, ulcerative colitis, etc. diseases in later life	Prolonged lactational amenorrhoea helps regain her strength
Hyper-natraemic dehydration etc. are avoided	-

Lessens tendency of growing obese in later childhood	Lowers incidence of breast cancer
Leads to proper formation of facial contour, jaw and mouth	Helps regain pre-pregnancy figure by stimulating fat metabolism
Imparts self-confidence and sociability	-

If mother takes inappropriate diet, it disturbs metabolism of the baby and leads it to serious diseases like *aruchi* (anorexia), *kaasa* (coughing), *shvaasa* (dyspnea), *hikkaa* (hic-cough), *tandraa* (drowsiness), *shoola* (colic pain), *kushtha* (obstinate skin problems), *gulma* (abdominal growths), *rakta-pitta* (bleeding problems), *shosha* (consumption), *galagraha* (obstruction in throat), *moha* (loss of consciousness), *unmaada* (insanity), *graha roga* (diseases caused by affliction of typical micro-being groups described elaborately in *Ayurveda*), etc. which not only disturb its growth and development but may cause permanent impairment or death.

Maatru Paricharyaa (Holistic care of the neo-mother):
First three days:
Paricharyaa (Care taken):
Clean genitals with warm water.
Observe colour, quantity and quality of lochia.
All that re-vitalizes and re-energizes the mother is done with utmost care.
She is gently massaged with warm Sesamum oil especially over abdomen, back, flanks, lumber region and both legs.
Clean and fumigated thick, strong, cotton cloth bandage is tied over abdomen.
Vagina is fumigated with dried cow dung and cow's *ghee*.
She is given enough rest and sleep in the *Prasootaagaara*.
Clean, cheerful and friendly environment free from noise, hustle and lights is maintained.
A whole body bath is avoided to prevent fatigue.

Aahaara (Food and water):
Give only boiled water to drink.
Give freshly made jaggery water with *Panchakola* [*Sunthi* (Zingiber officinale), *Mari* (Piper nigrum), *Pippali* (Piper longum), *Pippali mula* (root of Piper longum) and *Chitraka* (Plumbago Zeylanica)] powder and cow's *ghee* early morning and evening empty stomach, after placental expulsion.

Give *Yavaagu* made in *ghee*.

Avoid giving heavy recipes as diet (*halvaa, shiraa, laddu*); dry, fried, spicy, fermented, preserved, refrigerated foods. Avoid even regular family food. Try to give rest to the digestive system yet maintain nutritional status. Compensate the fluid loss incurred during and post-delivery with plenty of fluids (she is able to take).

From the time she feels hungry on day one, she is given decoction of *Kulattha* (Dolichos biflorus) as per her in-take capacity.

Aushadha: (Medicines):

Decoction of *laghu-panchmoola* is given with oil (in case of male child) or *ghee* (in case of female child).

Give *Shunthi* (Zinziber officinale) and *Harde* (Terminalia chebula) with jaggery twice a day.

Management during day IV to VII:
Paricharyaa (Care taken):

Same as stated above.

She is given simple body bath with heated water on day IV.

Aahaara (Food and drinks):

Only boiled water is given for drinking when she feels thirsty.

Give *Yavaagu* with oil, *ghee* along with salt as per taste or milk.

Give *Yava, Kola, Kulattha* baked with rice

Give vegetables like *Kushmaanda* (winter gourd), *Moolaka* (Radish), *Surana* (Amorphophallus paeoniifolius) etc. prepared in *ghee*.

Diet selected is based upon digestive capacity of mother; quality and quantity of lactation which can be known from the behaviour, urine and stool of the baby.

Aushadha (Medicines):

Same as stated above.

Management during day VII to XII:
Paricharyaa (Care taken):

Same as stated above.

She is given body and head bath with heated water on day XI or XII.

Aahaara (Food and drinks):

Only boiled water is given for drinking.

Yusha of *Yava*, *Kola* or *Kulattha* is given with easy to digest nutritive food.

Shaali rice dominant family diet is preferred.

Those having good appetite and a positive family non-vegetarian diet habit, may start with light to digest recipes while constantly monitoring self and baby for signs of proper-digestion.

Aushadha: (Medicines):

Same as stated above.

Medicines that control *vaayu* and revitalize mother are used.

Oil (in case of male child) or *ghee* (in case of female child) is used in making food, massage etc. This is related with hormonal status of mother and through her milk the baby.

Drugs of *Jeevaniya*, *Brumhaniya* and *Madhura* groups are used along with oil or *ghee* for whole body mother massage and with food for mother.

End of first phase of the post-natal period.

Management from day XIII to XXX

(i.e. completion of I month of *Sootikaa kaala*):

Paricharyaa (Care taken):

Same as stated above.

Give enough whole body and local hot fomentation.

Continue use of hot water for bath and boiled water to drink.

She has to take care and avoid fatigue, strain, anger, cold and dampness.

Vaginal canal is protected from *vaayu,* inflammation and infection by *dhoopa* and using sterile cotton cloth pads.

She is given body and head bath with heated water on day XXI.

Aahaara (Food and drinks):

Same as stated above.

End of phase II of the post-natal period.

Physiology of breast feeding:

Four stages are essential for normal breast feeding:

1) Mammogenesis: Proper development of the milk producing tissue
2) Lactogenesis: Initiation of milk production

3) Galactopoiesis: Maintenance of lactation
4) Galactokinesis: Ejection reflex

These stages occur as a result of hormonal actions and interactions. The main hormone Prolactin is directly related to neurogenic impulses from conditional stimuli i.e. seeing the child (vision reflex), feeling the child in arms or at breast (touch reflex), hearing voice of the child (sound reflex) and body odour of the baby (smell reflex) along with the baby's sucking at nipples and coaxing the breasts. Even remembering the child can lead to lactation in a mother having due feelings for her baby.

Adverse psychological factors can inhibit this flow and even suppress lactation.

Once lactation is established, a steady flow can be assured by regular emptying of breasts. It can be by baby sucking or manual removal.

Try to avoid use of breast pump.

Management after VI week till baby learns to crawl and teething starts:

Dhaatri paricharyaa (Lactating mother after onset of menstrual cycle):

A healthy mother with a healthy baby; having good digestion and no symptoms of *vaata* vitiation; is slowly brought back to normal (before conception) state and healthy routine.

Practice abstinence strictly at least till child completes six months of age.

Practice baby centric behaviour in accordance to changing seasons.

Avoid staying in or going to places having strong winds, heat or cold, high humidity or sudden change in temperatures or environment. It brings sudden chemical changes in yet not strong enough body. Baby requires time up-to completion of its first birthday to get strong enough to adjust and maintain health in varied atmospheres.

Avoid physical stress and emotional upsets.

Avoid journeys.

Avoid staying away from the baby or keeping baby alone.

End of post-natal period (*Sootikaa kaala*) of mother and total dependency on maternal milk of baby.

The baby is put on weaning only after it is able to sit independently, crawls with ease and teething has initiated.

General properties and effects of six seasons and six food tastes on human body:

Season	Shishira	Vasant	Grishma	Varsha	Sharad	Hemant
Nature of season	Cold Dry	Cold but pleasant Pollens etc. allergens	Hot Dry Windy	Humid Cold	Hot Humid Pollens etc. allergens	Pleasant cold Humid
Dominant tastes	Sweet salty Sour	Bitter Chilly Astringent	Sweet Bitter astringent	Sweet Sour Salty	Sweet Bitter Astringent	Sweet Sour Salty
Nature	Hot Oily	Hot Dry	Cold Oily	Hot Oily	Cold Dry	Hot Oily
Resultant effect on *dosha*	*Kapha* starts accumulating	*Kapha prakopa pitta shaman*	*Kapha shaman Vaayu* accumulation	*Vaayu prakopa Pitta* accumulation	*Vaayu shaman Pitta prakopa*	*Kapha* accumulation
Effect on body energy status	Maximum energy	Energy lessening	The least energy	Energy starts accumulating	Energy status very low	Energy status improving

CHAPTER 6

Nava-jaata paricharyaa [Neo-nate care]

Importance:

Child is a combined representation of each cell, part, system and mind-set of its parents. This makes clear that it is for the parents to see that they give a healthy, happy, prosperous and satisfying life to the child they have brought into the world.

Birth-rituals are followed all over India. It is understood that they leave life-long effects.

Nava-jaata paricharyaa [Neo-nate care] is divided into three phases:
1) *Jaatamaatra* (till its cord is pulsating) *paricharyaa*
2) *Sadya-jaata* (phase between stoppage of cord pulsations and cord trimming) *paricharyaa*
3) *Nava-jaata* (life after cord trimming up-to age 45 days) *paricharyaa*

Important steps of *Jaatakarma* (birth-rituals):
- **Praana pratyaagamana** (revival of consciousness):

  Fetus faces severe strain while passing through the birth canal and getting born. It often takes some time to gain consciousness. Sometimes the initiation of breathing is delayed. Hence some measures have to be applied for initiating and stabilizing consciousness and rhythmic breathing.

  There are three main steps:

  (1) Strike two smooth heavy stones (*ashmano snghattanam karnayo moole*) near the right ear of male and left ear of female child (auditory stimulation).

  (2) If child does not respond, splash with hand, hot and cold water alternately on the child (touch stimulation).

  (3) If both above measures fail, the child is fanned with a fan made from bamboo stem or a grain-cleaner (*surpa*) made from black grass (*krishna kapaalikaa*) till it gets properly resuscitated (auditory and touch stimulation).

Nowhere in *Ayurveda* beating, furling or hanging head low of the neonate is mentioned. Practice says they are not needed. A healthy baby starts normal activities the moment it touches the external environment and human hands. Yet certain steps are to be observed mandatorily to ensure sustained health of the neo-nate.

- **Mukha aadi baahya chidra smshodhana** (cleansing the external orifices):
  Fetus in its intra-uterine life remains covered with a sticky material to protect the skin from effect of contact with amniotic fluid. During the stress and strain faced during labour, the vernix and sometimes meconium stains the eyes, nose, mouth, tongue and throat. This hinders baby's immunity and recovery speed. Hence they need to be removed at the earliest. They are manually removed by an expert. The nail paired small finger-tip is covered with sterile cotton gauze and each orifice is cleaned gently with aseptic precautions.

- **Ulbaapanayana**:
  During parturition, there is a possibility of the foetus swallowing amniotic fluid along with skin cells, hair, urine, meconium etc. which are harmful to its digestive system. These have to be removed smoothly and effectively from the digestive tract. So *Saindhav*a (rock salt) salt (a grain amount) mixed with *ghee* (two drops) is given orally to the neonate. It acts as a mild emetic but some-times leads to only passing of meconium stained stool. Both the ways it cleanses the gut. It is an immuno-protective procedure hence some prefer to call it a *samsakaara*.

- **Naabhi-kalpana** (cord trimming):
  Umbilical cord is held carefully after it stops throbbing. A mark is made and tightly bond at 2 inches and 4 inches from the naval root. The umbilicus is trimmed delicately, with sterilized sharp instrument, having a curve with sharp edge on its inner side (*Ardha dhaara* or *Mandalaagra*), made from gold, silver or iron. *Naabhi-kalpana* is carried out only after thoroughly tying the cord at both sites (baby and maternal), with sterile (silk or cotton) thread. The cord stump is dressed, taking all aseptic precautions with warm medicated oil (*Kushtha*, *Balaa* or *Nirgundi*), maintaining its upright position. The upright position of cord helps stop extra oozing. The application

of warm oil is to cure inflammation and ease pain which promotes healthy and in time healing. It has been observed that the desired quality of healthy skin cells take up place easily in the umbilical wound. Inappropriate handling, cutting or dressing of the cord or its wound leads to various categories of intestinal prolapses in the natural naval cavity or suppuration due to infection. In both cases, the child suffers. Achieving this mile-stone requires deftness which is signified by the term *kalpana* i.e. trimming and not *kartana* i.e. cutting.

- Oral cavity is cleaned with smooth wetted sterile cotton cloth.

- *Madhu* (honey) and *ghee* (in unequal proportion) are administered (in dose of 2 drops *madhu* and 1 drop *ghee* every 30 to 45 minutes) till mother is relaxed and ready to feed the initial milk (colostrum called *Piyusha* in *Ayurveda*).

- Baby is massaged with medicated (*Balaa*) oil; given bath with *Sarvagandha* or Aromatic group of drugs known for their immuno-protective, antimicrobial, antifungal and skin health ensuring properties. Those who can afford are given bath with heated gold or silver immersed water.

- Baby is dried and draped properly keeping its hands and legs in a straight position in previously used soft silk or cotton cloth which is clean and adequately fumigated. This draping the baby in cloth gives it comfort and helps it gain height in future.

- The neo-father chants pious *mantra* and himself gives first feeding of *Jaatakarma* i.e. honey with *ghee* and spot-full of gold leaf (total quantity not exceeding the hollow of baby's right hand palm) approximately 2 to 3 drops.

- Baby when gets hungry on the day of birth, is given *Piyusha* (means nectar, *Ayurveda* term for colostrum).

A special procedure is performed: The neo-father taking the draped baby in his arms requests wife to feed his child from her breasts, which are abundant with milk. Though a very small procedure, it has a long-lasting psychological impact.

- Baby is first fed according to its sex. Right breast is given first to a male and left to the female child. This is in accordance with the *Idaa* (Sun) and *Pingalaa* (moon) *naadi* theory of strength. Before giving feed, the initial 2 to 3 drops are manually expressed by mother to avoid *kapha* vitiation in the child. Once lactation gets stabilized, baby is fed on only its mother's milk (*maatureva peebet stanyam tat parama deha vrudhdhaye*). Initial every feed comes from the reservoir which means it remained stagnant for some time. Stagnant milk is dominant in *kapha dosha* which causes indigestion to the baby. Indigestion is always a cause of disease which is a costly affair for a neo-nate.

- Cotton pad soaked in *Balaa taila* (medicated oil of Sida cordifolia Linn.) is put over the vertex (mid-skull) portion of the baby's head and tied softly with a cotton gauze band passing under its chin which maintains the pad in place till it gets dried by itself.
  This manoevre removes any effects of injury to the central nervous system inflicted during labour or during post-natal baby care and protects from any ill-effects here-after.

- An earthen pot filled with water is put at the head side of the child's cradle.
  It pacifies the central nervous system and ensures its proper functioning and promotes undisturbed sleep.

- Neonate constantly stays close to its mother and under expert observation. It remains well protected from cold, direct light, loud and harsh voices, wind, dampness, insects, animals, microbes, evil eyes etc. any-thing and every-thing that can cause harm.

- The room is fumigated with *dhoopana* drugs three times a day. The temperature and dryness are maintained by a constantly burning wood-fire.

- The clothes, beddings, furnishings of mother and child are always fumigated before use.

- Neonate and its mother are kept completely isolated and under constant expert observation for the initial and crucial ten days.

- Mother takes her first head bath on eleventh day post-delivery.

- Mother is kept on strict diet till she feeds baby i.e. up to baby's age of one year.

- Child's routine remains the same till its age thirty days.

- On completion of first month of life, on an auspicious clear day and constellation, the child is bathed and taken out of room to visit the family Deity. This is the *Nishkramana Samsakaara.*

The first crucial phase in a child's post-birth life is thus over.

The management is a much specialised one and requires an experienced, expert *Kaumaarabhrutya* (neonatologist having expert knowledge of natal and post-natal cares) to take care at each step, each hour and day.

Dhaatri parikshaa (Essential qualities of a feeding mother):

'*Mamma*' or "*Ma*" is a Latin word. Breasts or Mammary glands are secondary sex organs in a female designed to provide ready, healthy nutrition to its new-born.

Ayurveda has a clear concept of emotional bonding between mother and child. It does not even advocate spoon maternal milk feeding. In very exceptional cases goat's milk is given. In absence of even that cow's milk is given after adding proportionate water, sugar, heating it and then given to the child under strict observation.

A few of the qualities of a feeding mother are given here:
Physical qualities:
- Middle aged
- Has same body color as child
- Is neither too fair nor too dark in complexion
- Has a good physique
- Is neither too thin nor too obese
- Has neither too many hair nor very sparse hair
- Is free from chronic or infective disease
- Does not have defect in any limb
- Has excellent breast shape i.e. neither too big or small, neither directed upwards or dangling, neither long or short; nipple is smooth and placed in middle of the breast. In short they should be such that the child is able to suck without any effort. The shape of the maternal breast and position of baby while feeding

are responsible for the shape of the baby's lips, jaw and face; its satisfaction and health.

- There is enough and easy milk out-put; child does not have to strain.
- Her looks are good i.e. not terrifying to the child (if she is not its mother)

Psychological qualities:
- Is steady in thoughts
- Is good natured
- Always remains cheerful
- Is well mannered
- Likes cleanliness and keeps clean
- Cares and has feelings for the child
- Observes celibacy
- Does not get lured, is not greedy
- Is not lazy
- She does not speak or laugh loudly
- Does not mix with people doing wrong work
- Does not have vices like tobacco, wine, drugs, betting, etc.
- Knows and is skillful in child upbringing

Social status:
- Belongs to same caste, clan and community as the child
- Is born in the same land as the child
- Has alive healthy child of same age and sex

The nurse who is bereaved, hungry, tired, pregnant, having any long standing disease, fever, having too long breasts, breasts with nipple facing upwards, who is not able to control herself from over eating, different emotional upsets, cannot maintain celibacy, etc.; who always keeps on complaining should not feed a child as she brings different diseases to the fed.

Shyaamaa is the choicest type of wet nurse.

How to recognize *Shyaamaa*?

She remains warm during winter (*sheeta kaale bhavet ushnaa*) and cool during summer (*grishme cha sukha sheetalaa*); her skin colour is like molted gold (*tapt kaanchana varnaabhaa, saa stri Shyaamaa iti kirtitaa*) and she gives profuse amount of milk (*dogdhree*).

Shudhdha stanya (Excellence of quality and quantity of breast milk):
The sign is: baby grows well, completes the growth and development landmarks in time and does not face any problems or diseases related with breast milk.

Kumaaraagaara: [The place where a child dwells]
Today we name it as the children's room.

Even in a house where such convenience is not possible, a corner is always there where a child's belongings, clothes, toys etc. are kept neatly.

Ayurveda guides on this point and that can be practiced at home, school, clinic or hospital ward also.

A child (up to age 12 months) should not be exposed to external atmosphere, known or unknown hands, things which it dislikes or shuns away from, etc.

Unhindered growth and development of a child should be the prime concern of family and society.

Place or location:
The place selected should be cheerful, pleasant, devoid of loud unfriendly noises. It should contain a kitchen, storeroom, lavatory, bathroom, bedroom, and playroom and so on. The plan and construction should be in accordance with the *Vaastu Shaastra* rules.

There should be a properly made water reservoir with a covering to ensure water quality.

Kumaaraagaara should be properly ventilated such that the sunrays do not fall directly nor does the eastern wind enter the room or building directly. *Kumaaraagaara* should not be easily accessible for insects, rodents, wild animals and other harmful beings. The premises and rooms remain comfortable during all seasons and climate changes. Care should be taken that it remains devoid of humidity, dampness, unfriendly smell, darkness in all seasons.

There should be a place where prayers are offered regularly. Proper fumigation with sesame seeds, mustard seeds, *Guggulu* (Commifora mukul), should be done regularly.

An experienced *Kaumaarbhrutya* i.e. *Vaidya* having expertise in child related things, a servant who has affection for the child and is an expert in child-upbringing (*Kumaaraadhaara*), an experienced servant (*parichaaraka*), female servant (*parichaarikaa*), an experienced elderly caring relative have to remain present constantly.

Furniture:

The bed, seat, chair, table etc. should be made from child friendly material such that it remains comfortable in all seasons.

Kreedaa bhumi (mud play-ground):

Should be even, not having thorns, pebbles, stones etc. which may hurt a child. It should be sprinkled with medicated decoctions to enhance aseptic conditions and remove harmful insects. An experienced, child caring adult keeps a constant watch on the child while it is playing.

Kreedanakaani (toys)

The toys of a child are pleasing, having pleasant sound, light weighted, do not have sharp point or sharp edge, are not too small as to enter the child's mouth, made from child friendly material, the shape does not cause fear in it's mind. The toys stimulate the senses, are propioceptive and interactive.

Age-wise diet required for proper growth and development of a child:
A child is classified according to the type of food it takes post-birth:

1) *Ksheerapa baala*: only milk fed up to 12months. While up to 6mts only breastfed

2) *Ksheeraannaada baala*: milk with added cereals, pulses; seasonal fruits, etc. up to 24 months

3) *Annaada baala*: slowly brought to regular family diet from age of 25 months

Ayurveda Immunization and Specific Diet:

- Before birth (through mother): *Phala ghruta, Medhya Rasaayana Churna*

- At birth: *Suvarna praashana*—administering pure gold metal when child is hungry, taking all aseptic precautions.

- After 45 days: *Suvarna praashana, Medhya Rasaayana Churna*

- After *Anna praashana Samskaar: Preenana modaka*

- After 12 months: *Preenana modaka + Laghu vasanta maalati*

- After 5 years: *Preenana modaka + Suvarna Brahmi vati + Arvindaasava*

- 16 years: *Suvarna Brahmi vati + Arvindaasava + Ashtmangala ghrita*

CHAPTER 7
Signs of a healthy child and adult

[Observe after the '*naamakarana samsakaara*' i.e. naming ceremony]

There are certain signs which are generally observed after the child starts walking, talking, having varied social acquaintances and on maturity. *Ayurveda* advocates observing them since birth. Some of these signs are put here for the sheer cause of knowledge that this is also to be observed by the parents and elders.

The points put here are only a few and amongst those generally observed.

The only reason for putting this list here is to create a general awareness in terms of healthy growth and development of a child.

Head: Circumference is a little larger but is consistent with the body frame.

Hair: Are abundant, each hair follicle is clear, distinct, smooth, deep, black. The scalp skin is even, thick, smooth, and red in colour. It does not have abrasions or wounds.

Fore head: Prominent, clear, even, big (own 4 fingers), with good bony joints, properly covered by muscles from all sides, has transverse lines.

Ears: Large, thick, pinna even (measures own 4 fingers), lobes big, smooth, external-meatus has adequate and clear lumen.
They are properly and evenly placed i.e. in line with the temporal end of the eyes.

Eye brows: Slightly curved, do not get mingled in the midline, are equal, thick and long (own 4 fingers).

Eyes: Even, equal, having equal vision, evenly placed, lowered, having steady sight, having natural glow. The white and black parts are proportionate and clearly differentiated.

Eye lids: Beautiful and have clear and distinct nasal and temporal joints.

Nose: Sharply curved, habit of deep breathing, prominent bridge, apex is a bit lowered, length own 4 fingers.

Mouth: Straight, evenly prominent, aperture adequate; teeth are of proper colour, shape and size. Teething should be timely and in the proper sequence.

Lips: Neither too thick nor too thin, properly curved, properly covering the mouth, red in colour, length own 4 fingers.

Tongue: Proper length and breadth, smooth, soft, supple, thin, has natural whiteness and redness.

Palate: Smooth, properly toned, warm, red in colour.

Voice: Loud, strong, smooth, echoing, deep and effective.

Chin: Big, prominent (own 4 fingers).

Neck: Rounded, not too broad. Joint where neck meets chest should not be prominent.

Shoulders: Should be smooth, well-toned and strong. They should not be lean or thick. The male has broad straight shoulders. The female has drooping but strong shoulders.

Chest: Broad in male-own 24 fingers corresponds to the breadth of female pelvis. Female has chest breadth of 16 fingers which corresponds the male pelvis.

Chest flanks: Rounded, properly covered with muscles, muscles properly toned, smooth, soft, not having prominent veins, devoid of hair.

Back: Broad at the upper end, smooth, even, not having prominent veins, devoid of hair, mid part of the back (vertebral column) is slightly below the plane of the back.

Vertebrae: Should be properly covered with muscles.

Buttocks: Round, short, smooth, equal in size and shape, devoid of hair and wounds.

Dimple over the buttocks: Deep, equal, properly shaped, devoid of hair or having sparse hair directing to the right.

Abdomen: Slightly bulging, toned, even, having 3-4 transverse lines.

Naval: Big, deep, border is prominent, devoid of hair or veins. Naval is shaped like a coil bending towards the right side.

Abdominal flanks: Prominent, smooth, even, devoid of hair and prominent veins.

Pelvic region: Should be properly covered with muscles. Breadth in a male is 16 own fingers, in a female 24 own fingers.

Penis: Proper shape, size, colour, head proper in shape, lumen of adequate size.

Scrotum: Equal, proper size and colour.

External female genitalia: Proper shape, size, colour.
In adult: lips symmetrical, smooth, devoid of boils, thickening etc. Pubic hair-smooth, facing upwards (not going downwards), hair line not prominent.
Perineum: devoid of hair.

Urinary meatus: Clear lumen, well defined margin, proper shape.

Urine flow: Urine should flow evenly, straight, with due force. The passage of urine should be smooth, without any other odour (other than urine), burning, pain, heat, other colour i.e. other than straw colour, without irritation, without any sound.
In a female: coincides with all points of male except that it flows out diffusely (not in the form of straight flow like male).

Anal orifice: Properties resemble the naval.

Axillae (arm pit): Adult female should have less hair

Arms: Thick (having enough muscle mass), long (up-to knees), joints not demarkable (properly covered by muscles). Adult male has thick hair and some prominent veins

Wrist joints: 1 to 7 straight, deep, smooth, prominent, unbroken transverse lines on the inner side of joint. Has proper articulation. Male has a fat broad joint. Female has a thin, delicate looking joint.

Thighs: Proper length, muscles adequately toned, skin smooth, veins not prominent.

Knee joints: Proper articulation and properly covered with muscles.

Leg calves: Properly toned, devoid of thick profuse hair, veins not prominent.

Ankles: Small, joint properly covered by muscles, devoid of hair, veins not prominent.

Feet: Proper in shape, size and well-toned.

Feet soles: Red, shinning, have *urdhva rekha* (line going along direction of fingers), *swastika*, *hala* (plough), *padma* (lotus), *shankh*a (conch), and *chakra* (wheel) etc. auspicious signs.

Heels: Shining properly rounded and smooth.

Nails: Of both hands and feet: shinning, thin, smooth, naturally long, rounded ends, prominent like the back of a tortoise, copper red, have straight vertical lines.
Gait (walking style): like a cheerful elephant, bull, lion, tiger or swan; steady, unhurried and confident.
A child whose various activities like smiling, crying, sucking breast, sleeping, waking, voiding, passing flatus, urinating, trying to do something new etc. are very natural i.e. done without effort, whose tendons, veins, joints are properly covered by toned muscles; body parts and organs are strong and attractive; the sensory and performing organs are steady is healthy.

There are many other auspicious and good properties inherited.

There are eight types of *Saatvika* properties. Same way there are *Rajas*, *Tamas*, dual and *Shudhdha Satva* also.

Properties of *Shudhdha Satva*: health, in depth knowledge, peace, personality, prolonged life span, living happily and enjoying earthly pleasures.

In short, shape of face coincides with the behavior or personality, the eyes with the mind, the voice with the body strength, the looks with the nature of the person.

Conclusion or Fruit of this churning:

"Deerghajeevitamaarogyam dharmarthm sukhm yashah
Paathaavbodhaanushthanaihi adhigachantyo druvam" ||82||
[A. H. U. 40]

It says that following the rules of healthy living and life-style gives long life span, ensures health; maintains auspiciousness, economic steadiness, brings in happiness and fame, knowledge of path to good life and life after.

In short it brings in all the earthly and spiritual wealth a person seeks.

Aacharya Charaka in his text has used these words which explain why all these details, labour, expenses, stress are to be bore by the family, the physicians and society as a whole:

"Putrashisham karma samrudhdhi karakam,
yadukta metad mahadarthasamhitam
tadacharan kno vidbhihi yatha tatham
poojam yatheshtam labhate anasuyaka"

He says a healthy child is a treasure; it is being brought to the earth by following a strict protocol (mentioned earlier).

A human child is different from an animal, bird, insect or any other living being in the universe.

All the texts of *Ayurveda* have emphasized unanimously on this point.

This treasure of India needs to be made as much common as possible in the larger interest of human race.

Ayurveda defines health as (accepted by W. H. O.):

**"Sama doshah sama agnihi cha sama dhaatu malakriyaihi
Prasanna Aatmaa Indriya Mana Swashtha iti abhidhiyate"**

"A holistically healthy child has physiologically balanced body *dosha*, digestive power and *dhaatu* with proper excretion of *mala;* has maintained bliss of *Aatmaa, Indriya* and *Mana.*"

By **going through** this often,

By **understanding** this

By **implementing** this

A human being
Gains:
- ➢ Long life—*Deerghjeevita*
- ➢ Health—*Aarogya*
- ➢ Fulfillment of duties—*Dharma*
- ➢ Wealth—*Artha*
- ➢ Satisfaction—*Sukha*
- ➢ Social acceptance—*Yasha*

[*Ashtaanga Hridaya*]

"Child is the father of Man"

BIBLIOGRAPHY

- *Charak Samhitaa,* Dr Ram karan Sharma & Vaidya Bhagwan Dash, Chowkhamba Sanskrit Series office, Varanasi, II Edition, 1985
- *Charak Samhitaa* Commentary of *Yadavji Trikamji Acharya,* Chaukhamba Surbharti Prakashan, Varanasi, reprinted 2005
- *Sushruta Samhitaa, Shaastri Kalidaasa Govindji, Sastu Saahitya* Publication, Ahmedabad, IV Edition, 1974
- *Sushruta Samhitaa,* Commentary of Dr Bhaskar Govind Ghaanekara, Meharchand Lachmandas, I Edition, 1977
- *Ashtaanga Hridaya* Commentary of Vijayshankara Dhanshankara Munshi, *Sastu Saahitya* Publication, Ahmedabad II Edition, 1972
- *Ashtaanga Sangraha,* Commentary by Pandit Laalachandra Shaastri, Shri Baidyanath Ayurveda Bhavan Pvt. Ltd., I Edition, 1988
- *Shaalangadhara Samhitaa,* Commentator Vaidyshri Rasiklal Jethaalal Parikh, *Sastu Saahitya* Publication, Ahmedabad, IV Edition, 1981
- *Haarita Samhitaa,* Commentator Pandit Harihar Prasad Tripathi, Chaukhamba Krushnadas Academy, Varanasi, I Edition 2005.
- *Kaashyapa Samhitaa,* Commentator Shastri Girijaashankara Mayaashankara, *Sastu Saahitya* Publication, Ahmedabad, I Edition, 1970
- *Kaashyapa Samhitaa,* Commentary of Dr. P. V. Tewari, Chaukhambha Vishvabharati, Varanasi, 1996
- *Baal Tantrum* Dr Purushottamalal Menaria, Rajasthan Oriental Research Institute, Jodhpur 1972
- *Kaumarbhrutyam* Prof. Dr Nirmala Raajwade, Lokmanya Tilak Ayurveda College, Pune
- *Prasuti Tantra Stri Roga* Part I & II Dr Prof P V Tevari, BHU, Varanasi
- *Kaumarbhrutyam* Prof. Dr. P V Tevari, BHU, Varanasi
- *Kaumarbhrutyam* Prof. Dr. Dinesh K. S. V. P. S. V. Ayurveda College, Kottakal, Kerala

- *Kaumarbhrutyam* Prof. Dr. D. M. Pandya, Govt. Akhandanand Ayurveda College, Ahmedabad, Gujarat
- *Shubha santati yoga prakaasha,* Compiled by Pandit Ramprasaada Upadhyaaya, Shri Venkateshwara press, I Edition, 1965
- *Kaam sutra—Maharshi Vatsyayana*
- *Baal Tantram*—by *Raavana*
- *Shodasha Samskaar samuchchaya* compiled by Maharshi Vedvigyaana Academy, Ahmedabad, Gujarat
- *Kaya chikitsa* Part II Prof. Dr. Ajay Kumar Sharma, Rashtriya Ayurveda Sansthan, Jaipur, Rajasthan
- *Yoga Ratnaakara,* Commentary by Girijaashankar Mayaashankara Shaastri, *Sastu Saahitya* Publication, Ahmedabad, I Edition, 1971
- *Bhaava Prakaasha, Sastu Saahitya* Publication, Ahmedabad
- *Dravya guna vignaana* Part II-Prof. P. V. Sharma B. H. U., Chaukhambha Bharati, Academy, Varanasi, Reprinted 2011
- Embryology & Maternity in Ayurveda by Vd. Bhagwan Dash, Delhi Diary Publishers, New Delhi, I Edition, 1975
- *Purusha vichayah* Prof. V. J. Thakar, Gujarat Ayurveda University press, Jamnagar, I Edition 1984
- *Niraamaya Maatrutva,* Dr. K. Bhaskar Rav Translated by Dr. Minu Bhatt & Vaidya Bharati Joshi, Pro. P. K. Doshi Endowment, Mumbai, 1995
- *Bhaaratiya Samskaaro,* Prof (Dr) Bharati Kirtikumaar Shelat, Gujarat University Grants Board, II Edition, 2000
- Childhood, Maxim Gorky, Raguga Publishers, Moscow, Reprint 1984.
- Better Child Care, Dr. Bir Singh, Better Care Series, Voluntary Health Association of India, New Delhi.
- *Bhruna hatyaa mahaa paap!! bchavo bchaavo* Panyaas Rashmiratnavijaya, Jingun aaraadhak trust, Mumbai, IV Edition May 2007.
- Breast feeding with love for Third World Infants, Dr. B. N. Purandare, Dr. Mandakini Purandare, Dr. N. M. Purandare, Alarsin Pharmaceutical Publication, 1984.
- *Tame tamaaraa baalakne olkho,* Dr. Mohanbhai Panchal, Gala Publishers, II Edition, 1984.
- *Ayurveda anusaar sukhi evm swasth maatrutva,* Dr. P. V. Tevari, Dr. S. K. Sharma, National Academy of Ayurved, New Delhi.
- *Stri* (*Sandesh Prakashn*) Special issue, II Edition, May 1988.

- Revised History of Microbiology (Vedic to Modern), Dr. Chakradhar F, et al, RKVMRI, Vadodara, and Special Issue August 2007.
- Compilation of Interactive Workshop on *Prasuti tantra*, *Streeroga* & *Kaumara bhrutya*, November 2005, Rashtriya Ayurveda Vidyapeeth, New Delhi.
- Unani Medicine for Women, Dr. S. M. Hussain, Avicenna Research Publication, Mumbai, II Edition, March 2003.
- *Prasutitantra vijgnaana*, Dr. Jaymaalaa Shirke, Tathaagat Publication, III Edition, May 2011.

APPENDIX 1

Understanding *Ayurvedic* "**Kaumaarbhrutyam**"
[*Prasuti tantra* + *Stri roga* + *Baala roga* + *Baala dhaarana* + *Poshana*]
{Obstetrics + Gynecology + Neonatology + Paediatrics + Child Care + Nourishment}

Maternal	Health Care of to-be-Mother	Planned Parenthood
Antenatal Care	Infertility	Healthy Parents
Natal Care	Post-Delivery Problems	Healthy Conception
Post-Natal Care	Contraception	Healthy Birth
Care of wet mother	Other Problems	Healthy baby feeding
		Healthy baby-brought-up
		Healthy baby habits
Diseased stage:	**Infrastructure required:**	Room, toys,
Proper care at all stages	O.P.D. room	playground, Clothes,
	I.P.D. room	Class room
Infrastructure required:	Minor Operation Theatre	
O.P.D. Room	Emergency Room	Education building
Labour Room	*Panchakarmaagaara*	Entertainment facilities
Minor Operation Theatre	*Vaman kaksh*	
Operation Theatre	*Snehan kaksh*	**Infrastructure Required**
Emergency Room	*Svedana kaksh*	Post Natal Care Room
Waiting Room	*Basti kaksh*	Baby bath Room
Post Natal Ward	*Nasya kaksh*	Minor Operation Theatre
	Shirodhaaraa kaksh	*Panchakarmaagaara*
		Emergency Room
		Well Baby Clinic

APPENDIX 2

Eleven *Samsakaara*: (11 important steps to healthy offspring)

1) *Vivaaha samsakaara*:

It indicates completion of *Brahmacharyaashrama* and entry to *Gruhasthaashrama*. It creates awareness to responsibilities towards family, society, nation, nature etc. The conjugal life is primarily for a healthy child.

2) *Laaja homa* **and** *Putreshti yagna*:

The term '*putra*' indicates 'child'. Active procedure for a healthy child starts with the *Vivaaha samskaara* itself.

3) *Garbhaadhaana*:

Couple observes several rules and achieves pregnancy during a selected (*Nakshatra*) constellation (i.e. a planned pregnancy).

4) *Punsavana samsakaara* **or** *Straishuya Karma*:

Selection of sex and special regimes enhance genital potency of the child i.e. a child will be born with no congenital deficiencies in the genitals.

5) *Seemantonnayana samsakaara*:

It is a ceremony done only once in life. It is related with strongly anchoring the fetus during third trimester of first pregnancy. It also prepares the mother and family for the new arrival.

6) *Jaatakarma + Ulbaapanayana + Suvarna praashana samsakaara*:

It helps the new born quickly adjust, get accustomed and survive the extra-uterine atmosphere. It purifies the child of liqor amni etc. intake during birth and helps maintain immunity.

7) *Nishkramana samsakaara + Deva darshana + Naamkarana samsakaara + Shishu parikshanam*:

On completion of first month post-delivery, mother takes the sacred bath. Both mother and child go to their family god. The child comes into external environment (out of the *Kumaaraagaara*) for the first time. Naming ceremony is performed with the child in mother's lap, head in the east or north direction. Father offers prayers to the family deity and utters two names. One name is based on the birth constellation. The other name is the family or pet name. The official or first name should have a clear meaning, is similar to names of the family elders and is socially acceptable. Child is examined medically for any hidden problems. Some observe the *Nishkramana samsakaara* be done on completion of 4th month i.e. during the 5th month. That is more comfortable and advisable also.

8) *Upaveshana + Phalapraashana* (often misnamed *Anna praashana*)

Child is not given any type of food before its age of 12 months.

A child generally sits erect on completion of six months. Further development requires more nutrition hence seasonal fruit pulp crushed to paste is initiated ceremoniously. For the initial few days the amount of pulp given is a lick. Eruption of first molars in lower jaw is a definite indication of increasing digestive ability. Even then a child is given additive diet only if it is able to sit erect. In case even after completion of 6 months the child neither sits erect nor has teething then it is put on special diet along with medicines to enhance its growth. A seat is prepared for the *Phalapraashana* ceremony. An elevated structure is covered with cow dung. A soft seat made from silk material and covered with pillows on three sides so that the child seats comfortably is prepared. The place is decorated in a child-friendly way. Various toys are placed all around the seat for the child to play. Child is seated facing the east. It should not be allowed to seat at a stance for more than 48 minutes.

9) *Karnavedhana samsakaara*:

Lower part of the pinna of external ear contains a thinned out small part. It can be identified in sun-light. This part is pierced (taking all aseptic precautions) with a sharpened gold wire. It is generally done between 6-8 months age of child. It is an acupuncture point.

As per *Ayurveda* wearing ornaments maintains immunity and auspiciousness.

10) *Anna praashana Samsakaara:*

It is done on completion of 12 months age during the *Prajapatya* constellation. The child has developed teeth; is able to walk on its own. The grains selected and the food prepared for the *anna praashana samsakaara* is the family traditional food e.g. in a rice eating populace, *Shashthika Shaali* (rice that ripens in 60 days) are cooked in milk. When the rice becomes very soft, jaggery (red in colour and properly manufactured) is proportionately mixed. During the ceremony, only a lick of the mixture is given to the child. The dose is increased steadily under constant medical and elderly supervision. In no consequences is the child given unknown food. This *samsakaara* also indicates commencement of weaning.

11) *Upanayana samsakaara:*

Child is supposed to be able to express its likes, dislikes, feelings and needs clearly. It can understand and follow instructions. It knows the general rules and relations of its society. The holy-thread ceremony indicates starting of the first phase of social life viz. the *Brahmacharyaashrama*. Initially child learns to follow and obey the tough rules of *Gurukula* and then starts its education career. The role of the mother is now taken up by the teacher.

APPENDIX 3

Groups of useful drugs:

Single drugs
I—*Shramahara gana*:

Draakshaa (Vitis vinifera), *Kharjura* (Phoenix sylvestris Roxb.), *Priyaala* (Buchanania lanzan Spreng), *Badara* (Zyziphus jujube), *Daadima* (Punica granatum Linn.), *Anjeera* (Ficus carica Linn.), *Parushaka* (Grewia asiatica), *Ikshu* (Saccharum officinarum Linn.), *Yava* (Hordeum vulgare), *Shashtika* (Oriza sativa). (Ch. Su. 1/14)

These ten drugs energize a woman and help her throughout the antenatal, natal and postnatal period. They being food items are generally used as household remedy to fatigue.

II—*Prajaasthaapana gana*:

Aindri (Bacopa monnieri Linn Pennell), *Brahmi* (Centella asiatica Linn Urban), *Shataveerya* (*Shveta durvaa*, *Sahasraveerya* (Achyranthes aspera), *Amoghaa* (Stereospermum personatum), *Avyathaa* (Terminalia chebula), *Shivaa* (Terminalia chebula), *Arishtaa* (Fondaparinux sodium), *Vaatyapushpi* (Abutilon indicum Linn.).

(Ch. Su. 4/18)

These ten drugs help prevent abortion and should be a routine for every pregnant woman.

III—*Jeevaniya gana*:

Jivaka and *Rushabhaka* (Vidaarikanda, Pueraria tuberosa DC), *Medaa* and *Mahaamedaa* (*Shataavari*, Asparagus racemosus willd.), *Kaakoli* and *Ksheerakaakoli* (Roscoea procera wall.), *Mudgaparni* (Phaseolus trilobus Ait.), *Maashaparni* (Teramnus labialis Spreng.), *Jeevanti* (Leptadania reticulate W & A), *Yashtimadhu* (Glycyrrhiza glabra)

These ten drugs help prevent abortion. They should be made routine drugs for every pregnant woman. They are helpful in postnatal care specially feeding mothers; they prevent various diseases of postnatal period.

IV—*Balya gana*:

Aindri (Bacopa monnieri Linn Pennell), *Kapikachchu* (Mucuna prurita Hook.), *Shataavari* (Asparagus racemosus Willd.), *Maashaparni* (Teramnus labialis), *Kseeravidaari* (Ipomoea digitata), *Aswagandhaa* (Withania somnifera), *Shaalaparni* (Desmodium gangeticum DC.), *Rohini* (Dry rhizome with root of Picrorhiza kurroa Royle ex Benth), *Durva Shveta* and *Shyama* (Cynodon dactylon Pers.)

These ten drugs energize a woman and help her throughout the antenatal, natal and postnatal period. They being food items are generally used as household remedy to fatigue

V—*Kaakolyaadi gana*:

Kaakoli and *Ksheerakaakoli* (Roscoea procera wall.), *Jivaka* and *Rushabhaka* (*Vidaarikanda*, Pueraria tuberosa DC), *Mudgaparni* (Phaseolus trilobus Ait.), *Maashaparni* (Teramnus labialis Spreng.), *Medaa* and *Mahaamedaa* (*Shataavari*, Asparagus racemosus willd.), *Guduchi* (Tinospora cordifolia), *Karkatashrungi* (Pistacia integerrima Stewart ex Brandis), *Padmaka* (Nelumbo nucifera Gaertn.), *Mrudveekaa* (Vitis vinifera), *Jeevanti* (Leptadania reticulate W & A), *Madhooka* (Madhuca indica J. F. Gmel.). These drugs nullify the vitiated *Pitta*, *Vaayu* and *Rakta*. They increase the flow of breast milk (galactagogue) and have restorative, augment the virile potency in men.

Combinations of drugs:

I] *Phala ghruta*:

Triphalaa [powder of fruit bark of: *Haritaki* (Terminalia chebula), *Bibheetaka* (Terminalia bellirica Roxb.), *Aamalaki* (Emblica officinalis Gaertn.) in equal parts],

Sahachara (Nilgirianthus ciliates), *Guduchi* (Tinospora cordifolia), *Punarnava* (Boerhvia diffusa Linn.), *Shyonaaka* (Oroxylum indicum Vent.), *Haridra* (Curcuma longa Linn.), *Daaruharidra* (Berberis aristata DC.), *Raasanaa* (Pluchea lanceolata C. B. Clarke), *Shataavari* (Asparagus racemosus), milk, water—the decoction is boiled with cow's *ghee* to prepare *Phala ghruta*.

Dose: 10 to 30 grams once in morning empty stomach

Anupaana (vehicle): milk

Uses: It is administered to all women in the fertile period to maintain fertility, genital health; protect the foetus and pregnant woman; maintain mother and child health during lactation period.

II] *Devadaarvyaadi kwaatha*:

Devadaaru (Cedrus deodara), *Vachaa* (Acorus calamus Linn.), *Kushtha* (Saussurea lappa C. B. Clarke), *Pippali* (Piper longum Linn.), *Shunthi* (Zingiber officinale Rosc.), *Bhoonimba* (Andrographis paniculata Nees.), *Katphala* (Myrica esculenta Buch—Ham.), *Mustaa* (Cyperus rotundus), *Katuki* (Picrorrhiza kurroa), *Dhaanyaka* (Coriandrum sativum Linn.), *Haritaki* (Terminalia chebula), *Gajapippali* (Piper chaba Hunter), *Dhamaasaa* (Fagonia cretica), *Gokharu* (Tribulus terrestris), *Yavaasaa* (Alhagi camelorum Fisch.), *Bruhati* (Solanum anguivi), *Atisa* (Linum usitatissimum Linn.), *Guduchi* (Tinospora cordifolia), *Karkatashrungi* (Pistacia intergerrima Stewart ex. Branis), *Krishnajeeraka* (Carum bulbocastanum W. Koch.). These drugs are pastled to coarse powder and preserved in air-tight glass bottle. Fresh decoction is administered immediately after normal delivery twice a day up-to completion of *sootikaa kaala*.

Dose: 10 to 20 ml. twice daily

Anupaana (vehicle): honey, warm water

Uses: It protects her from pain, cough, fever, tremors, headache, excessive thirst, burning sensation, diarrhea and emesis etc. post natal problems.

III] *Dugdhavardhana churna*:

Vidaarikanda (Pueraria tuberosa), *Ashwagandhaa* (Withania somnifera), *Balaa* (Sida cordifolia) *seeds*, *Shataavari* (Asparagus racemosus) all drugs taken in equal parts (10), *Ativisha* (Aconitum heterophyllum) 2.5 parts, *Ikshumoola* (root of Saccharum officinarum), *Aamalaki* (Emblica officinalis; Indian gooseberry), *Taalamkhaanaa* (Astercantha longifolia) 5 parts and sugar 190 parts. All the ingredients are finely powdered and preserved in air-tight glass bottle.

Dose: 3 to 6 grams thrice a day

Anupaana (vehicle): honey, warm milk

Uses: ensures enough and healthy lactation. (Other precautions have to be observed).

IV] *Dashamoola kwaatha*:

Bilva (Aegel marmelos), *Gambhaari* (Gmelina arborea), *Shyonaaka* (Oroxylum indicum), *Kantakaari* (Solanum virginiana), *Bruhati* (Solanum anguivi), *Shaalaparni* (Desmodium gangaticum), *Prishniparni* (Uraria picta), *Arani* (Premna integrifolia), *Gokharu* (Tribulus terrestris), *Paatalaa* (Stereospermum suaveolens).

Roots of these ten herbs include *laghu* and *bruhat panchamoola*.

Dose: 10 to 20 ml. twice daily

Anupaana (vehicle): honey, warm water

Uses: in post-delivery weakness and fatigue; they pacify *vaata* and *kapha*; prevent and cure nervine disorders; give healthy sleep; are tonic to liver and kidneys; balance the hormones; clear gynaecological problems; have anti-inflammatory properties.

V] *Panchavalkala kwaatha*:

Vata (Ficus benghalensis Linn.), *Udumbara* (Ficus glomerata Roxb.), *Ashwattha* (Ficus religiosa Linn.), *Paarisha* (Thespesia populnea Soland ex Correa), *Plaksha* (Ficus lecor Buch. Ham) Stem barks of these five trees are used fresh or dried.

Dose: Internal: 10 to 20 ml. twice daily

External: 10 to 100 ml. as per need

Anupaana (vehicle): honey, warm water

Uses: They pacify *pitta* and *kapha*, disinfect wounds, have wonderful healing property, used in inflammatory and infective gynaecological disorders having discoloration or growths e.g. cervicitis, cervical erosion or excessive bleeding, burning, itching, etc.

VI] *Baalachaaturbhadra churna*:

Musta (Cyperus rotundus), *Pippali* (Piper longum), *Ativisha* (Aconitum heterophyllum), *Karkatashrungi* (Pistacia integerrima Stewart) are taken in equal parts, powdered finely and preserved in air-tight glass bottle.

Dose: 2 to 4 grains 2 to 4 times a day

Anupaana (vehicle): honey

Uses: Prevents and cures diarrhea, fevers, breathlessness, cough, emesis etc. The C. C. R. A. S., New Delhi has proved it to be a bitter tonic to children (day one to twelve year age).

The *Ayurvediya* texts have scores of such drugs which should be used only under expert observation.

APPENDIX 4

Hadlock fetal development chart:

Weeks	B. P. D. (mm)	H. C. (mm)	A. C. (mm)	F. L. (mm)
16	32.3	124.4	99.1	20.5
16.5	34.2	131.2	105.5	22.1
17	36.0	137.9	111.9	23.7
17.5	37.7	144.5	118.2	25.2
18	39.5	151.1	124.5	26.7
18.5	41.3	157.7	130.7	28.3
19	43.0	164.1	136.9	29.8
19.5	44.7	170.5	143.0	31.2
20	46.4	176.8	149.1	32.7
20.5	48.1	183.0	155.1	34.1
21	49.7	189.2	161.1	35.6
21.5	51.4	195.3	167.0	37.0
22	53.0	201.3	172.9	38.4
22.5	54.6	207.2	178.7	39.8
23	56.2	213.0	184.5	41.1
23.5	57.8	218.7	190.2	42.5
24	59.3	224.4	195.9	43.8
24.5	60.8	229.9	201.5	45.1
25	62.3	235.4	207.1	46.4
25.5	63.8	240.8	212.7	47.7
26	65.3	246.0	218.1	48.9
26.5	66.7	251.2	223.6	50.2
27	68.1	256.2	228.9	51.4

27.5	69.5	261.2	234.3	52.6
28	70.8	266.1	239.6	53.8
28.5	72.2	270.8	244.8	55.0
29	73.5	275.5	250.0	56.1
29.5	74.7	280.0	255.1	57.3
30	76.0	284.4	260.2	58.4
30.5	77.2	288.7	265.2	59.5
31	78.4	292.9	270.2	60.6
31.5	79.6	297.0	275.1	61.7
32	80.7	300.9	280.0	62.7
32.5	81.9	304.7	284.8	63.8
33	82.9	308.4	289.6	64.8
33.5	84.0	312.0	294.3	65.8
34	85.0	315.5	299.0	66.8
34.5	86.0	318.8	303.7	67.7
35	87.0	322.0	308.2	68.7
35.5	87.9	325.0	312.8	69.6
36	88.8	327.9	317.3	70.6
36.5	89.7	330.7	321.7	71.5
37	90.5	333.3	326.1	72.3
37.5	91.3	335.8	330.4	73.2
38	92.1	338.2	334.7	74.1
38.5	92.8	340.4	338.9	74.9
39	93.5	342.5	343.1	75.7
39.5	94.2	344.4	347.2	76.5
40	94.8	346.1	351.3	77.3
40.5	95.4	347.7	355.4	78.1
41	95.9	349.2	359.3	78.8
41.5	96.5	350.5	363.3	79.5
42	96.9	351.6	367.2	80.3

http://www.babymed.com/hadlock-estimated-measurements-weeks-gestation; 20/1/2013; 8:33pm

APPENDIX 5

Average height wise weight range of Indian women (aged 25 and above):

Height		Thin Structure	Normal Structure	Broad Structure
Cms.	Feet-Inch	Kgs.	Kgs.	Kgs.
147	4' 10"	42-44.5	43.5-48.5	47-54
150	4' 11"	42.5-46	44.5-50	48-55
152	5' 0"	43.5-47	46-51	49.5-56.5
155	5' 1"	45-48.5	47-52.5	51-58
158	5' 2"	46.5-50	48.5-54	52-59.5
160	5' 3"	47.5-51	50-55	53.5-61
163	5' 4"	49-52.5	51-57	55-62
165	5' 5"	50.5-54	52.5-58.5	57-64.5
168	5' 6"	52-56	54.5-61	58.5-66
170	5' 7"	53.5-57.5	56-63	60-68

(T.B. of *Yoga Praanaayaama* Dr. Babasaheb Ambedkar University, R. C. Patel Technical Institute, Ahmedabad)

APPENDIX 6

Creating a child-friendly environment at home, in school or community:

There are many plants, trees, creepers that create a positive atmosphere. These if planted and grown in and around the campus containing *Prasutaagaara, Kumaaraagaara,* school, collage, society hall, club, recreation or sports places, religious or historical spots; help create a friendly atmosphere. The need is for active social awareness: "Every child matters".

Sr. No.	Local name	Latin name	Type
1	*Vada*	Ficus benghalensis	Tree
2	*Pipal*	Ficus religiosa	Tree
3	*Paaraspipalo*	Thespesia populnea	Tree
4	*Ashoka*	Saraca asoca	Tree
5	*Umardo*	Ficus racemosa L.	Tree
6	*Galo*	Tinospora cordifolia	Creeper
7	*Vaasaa*	Adathoda vasica	Plant
8	*Shataavari*	Asparagus racemosus	Creeper/ Plant
9	*Yashtimadhu*	Glycyrrhiza glabra	Plant
10	*Jeevanti*	Leptadenia reticulate	Creeper
11	*Tulasi*	Ocimum tenuliflorum	Plant
12	*Bilva*	Aegle marmelos	Tree
13	*Ashwagandhaa*	Withania somnifera	Plant
14	*Vidaarikanda*	Ipomoea digitata	Plant
15	*Jai*	Jasminum grandiflorum/fluminense	Creeper
16	*Chameli*	Jasminum officinalae	Creeper
17	*Kamala*	Nelumbo nucifera	Plant
18	*Brahmi*	Bacopa monieri	Plant / Creeper
19	*Vachaa*	Acorus calamus	Plant
20	*Jataamaansi*	Nardostachys jatamansi	Plant

21	*Jiyaapotaa*	Putranjiva Roxburghii	Tree
22	*Shivalingi*	Bryonia laciniosa	Tree
23	*Durva*	Cynodon dactylon	Weed
24	*Saptaparna*	Alstonia scholaris	Tree
25	*Aamla*	Phyllanthus emblica	Tree
26	*Harde*	Terminalia chebula	Tree
27	*Bahedaa*	Terminalia belarika	Tree
28	*Naagarmotha*	Cyperus Rotundus	Tree
29	*Nagoda*	Vitex negundo	Middle sized tree
30	*Saarivaa*	Hemidesmus indicus	Plant
31	*Apaamaarga*	Achyranthes aspera	Plant
32	*Arjun*	Terminalia arjuna	Plant
33	*Fudino*	Mentha sylvestris Linn	Plant
34	*Tagara*	Valeriana wallichii	Plant
35	*Varuna*	Crataeva religiosa/nurvala	Tree
36	*Sarpagandhaa*	Rauvolfia serpentina	Plant
37	*Naagakesara*	Mesua ferrea	Plant
38	*Daaruhaldi*	Berberis aristata	Plant
39	*Gambhaari*	Gmelina arborea	Tree
40	*Kumaari*	Aloe vera	Plant
41	*Kalmegh*	Andrographis paniculata	Plant
42	*Manjishtha*	Rubia cordifolia	Plant
43	*Kadvo limdo*	Azadirachta indica	Tree
44	*Punarnavaa*	Boehavia diffusa	Plant
45	*Sadaabahaara*	Vinca rosea	Plant

A study reveals that trees not only clean the environment but add positivity and influence planetary effects believed by *Jyotisha shaastraa* (Astrology).

PRECONCEPTIONAL COUNCELLING MANAGEMENT PROFORMA

Name of the Centre (with Address):

Full name of participant: Serial number:

Postal address: Marriage life: Months/Years

Age: Husband: Yrs   Occupation: Husband: Noteworthy:

       Wife: Yrs   Wife:

Came for First Consultation: Date and Points:

Sr No	Date	Consultation Points	B.P.	Pulse	Menstruation Type L.M.P.	Vaginal Discharge	Urine	Stool	Appetite	Sleep & Dreams
1										
2										
3										
4										
5										
6										
7										
8										
9										
10										
11										
12										
Conclusion										

WELL BABY CLINIC PROFORMA

Name: Child: Age: D.O.B. Time: O.P.D.no
Father: Age: Occupation: Date & Time:
Mother: Age: Occupation: Doctor's Seal:
Postal Address: Birth History:

Contact Numbers (with names):
Chief complaint (with duration):

---

1. Pulse: /minute
2. Breathing: /minute
3. Temperature: ^{0}C/F
4. B.P.:   mmHg
5. Weight: Kgm
6. Height: Cm
7. Stool: /day;/night; Colour: Consistency:
8. Urine: /day;/night; Colour: Burning/Discharge/Itching
9. C.V.S.:
10. N.S.:   Reflexes:
11. Tongue: Coated: Colour: Pale/Pink/Spotted;
12. Throat:
13. Abdomen: General:
Liver:
Spleen:
14. Lymph-nodes:
Inguinal:
Cervical:
15. Nutritional Status:
16. Family History: Mother: Father:
Grand Fathers: M/P Grand Mothers: M/P
Sister: Brother: Others:
17. Diet:

Sociability:
Understanding:
Anything Noteworthy:
Investigations (with date):
Immunizations Completed (with date):

Advised:

Diet:
Suvarna Praashana:
Habits:
Exercises:

Sr. No	*Karma* (Procedures)	Drug to be used	Duration	Symptoms	
				B. T.	**A. T.**
1	*Abhyanga:Sarvaanga*				
	Ekanga				
2	*Svedana:ShashthiShaali*				
	NirgundiPatraPinda				
	Vaalukaa				
	Baashpa				
3	*Basti: Anuvaasana*				
	Aasthaapana				
	Maatraa				
	Ksheera				
4	*Shirodhaaraa*				
5	*Shirah pichchu*				
6	*Naasaa Purana*				
7	*Karna Purana*				
8	*Netra Purana*				
9	*Guda Pichchu*				
10	Other procedures (if needed)				

B. T.: Before Treatment
A. T.: After Treatment

SUVARNA PRAASHANA SHEDULE CARD

Full name of beneficiary: Serial No.

Postal address:

Date of I visit and advice given:

Sr. No	Date	Ht. In Cm	Wt. In Gm.	A. C.	C. C.	H. C.	Lt A. C.	Symptoms	Other
1									
2									
3									
4									
5									
6									
7									
8									
9									
10									
11									
12									

First date starts with *Pushya Nakshatra* day immediately post-birth

Abdominal Circumference (A. C.): taken at naval level

Chest Circumference (C. C.): taken at nipple level

Head Circumference (H. C.): taken at brow level

Left Arm Circumference (Lt. A. C.): taken at biceps bulge level

Other column is for changes (if any) noted after *Suvarna praashana*.

Which social body can contribute to this noble cause and how?

Voluntary Organizations	**Voluntary Action**	Youth Clubs
Corporate leaders		Co-Operatives
Panchaayats		Trade unions
Mahilaa mandala		Opinion leaders
Popular committees	**Community Participation**	Student communities
Village level volunteers		*Yuvaka Kendra*
Private practitioners		Elected Representatives
Youth clubs		Indian System Medical Practitioners

A child is not merely its parent's or family's responsibility, a healthy progeny can be achieved only with the whole society standing with the youth, specially to be parents, very specially to be mother.

The need of the hour is to put duties before rights in the interest of humanity and planet earth at large.

The author with folded hands most humbly, makes this request to all the readers to please donate their efforts to achieve this noble cause.

II *Bali Purushkaro hi Daivam tadapyanuvartate* II
"Destiny follows Strong human effort"